CREATIVE VARIATIONS IN THE
PROJECTIVE TECHNIQUES

Publication Number 387

AMERICAN LECTURE SERIES®

A Monograph in

AMERICAN LECTURES IN PSYCHOLOGY

Edited by

MOLLY HARROWER, Ph.D.

Professor of Research in Clinical Psychology
Department of Psychiatry
Temple University School of Medicine
Philadelphia, Pennsylvania

CREATIVE VARIATIONS in the
PROJECTIVE TECHNIQUES

By

MOLLY HARROWER, Ph.D.

Professor of Research in Clinical Psychology
Department of Psychiatry
Temple University School of Medicine

PAULINE VORHAUS, Ed.D.

Clinical Psychologist
Veteran's Administration
New York City

MELVIN ROMAN, Ph.D.

Research Consultant
Department of Psychiatry
Albert Einstein Medical College

GERALD BAUMAN, Ph.D.

Research Consultant
Department of Psychiatry
Albert Einstein Medical College

With a Foreword by
BRUNO KLOPFER

CHARLES C THOMAS • PUBLISHER
Springfield • Illinois • U.S.A.

CHARLES C THOMAS • PUBLISHER

BANNERSTONE HOUSE

301-327 East Lawrence Avenue, Springfield, Illinois, U.S.A.

Published simultaneously in the British Commonwealth of Nations by

BLACKWELL SCIENTIFIC PUBLICATIONS, LTD., OXFORD, ENGLAND

Published simultaneously in Canada by

THE RYERSON PRESS, TORONTO

With THOMAS BOOKS careful attention is given to all details of manufacturing
and design. It is the Publisher's desire to present books that are satisfactory as to
their physical qualities and artistic possibilities and appropriate for their particular
use. THOMAS BOOKS will be true to those laws of quality that assure a good name
and good will.

Printed in the United States of America

FOREWORD

Just twenty years ago Molly Harrower, the editor of this series, entered the field of projective techniques by participating in one of my first summer workshops, beginning in that way to establish herself in this chosen area as one of the "experts" in the country. One year later Pauline Vorhaus made the switch from the field of journalism to that of psychology and started on an increasingly rewarding career of work, teaching and publications.

It would have been difficult to publish a book like *Creative Variations* at that time. Projective techniques still needed another decade to establish themselves as part of the core curriculum of clinical psychology and as one of the most versatile tools of the clinician.

The recent development in the theoretical and methodological discussion, especially L. J. Cronbach's Presidential Address for the A.P.A. entitled "The Two Disciplines of Scientific Psychology," and, more recently, an article by Reuben Fine, "The Logic of Psychology," in *Psychoanalysis and the Psychoanalytic Review* (Volume 45, No. 4), have clarified the position of projective techniques and enable us to progress to more productive publications.

From their original purpose as a diagnostic adjunct, projective techniques have found their most useful application in the service of prognostic clarification. From there, it is only a short step to employ them at the same time as a point of departure for actual therapeutic measures.

Molly Harrower, with her "Projective Counseling," has done this in her usual ingenious way, both with individuals and groups.

Pauline Vorhaus, selecting as point of departure the Draw-a-Person procedure, compares in her "Structured Interview" what the subject says about the figure he draws and what he says about himself. Her elaborate case study exemplifies the possibilities of this technique amply, and would have been worth publishing by itself.

Melvin Roman and Gerald Bauman round out the picture with their "Interaction Testing," using the Rorschach and the WAIS as the basis for illustration.

It can only be hoped that this book will start clinicians to develop confidence in their technique and give them a variety of tools to make the logical step from diagnosis to therapy.

—BRUNO KLOPFER

CONTENTS

CREATIVE VARIATIONS IN THE PROJECTIVE TECHNIQUES

PROJECTIVE COUNSELING—
A PSYCHOTHERAPEUTIC TECHNIQUE

As psychologists we have been tending, in recent years, to forget our concern with the normal individual. So caught up have we become with the emotionally ill, so eager have we been to add our skills to the therapeutic armamentarium, that we have lost interest in the relatively well-adjusted. Yet many individuals who have undergone intensive forms of psychotherapy as a last resort have wondered whether the course of their lives might have been different had the same kind of self-understanding and insight been possible prior to the development of their acute distress.

Few people have the opportunity to know themselves, or to become aware of the distorting factors of their unconscious motivations. It is not until "things" go wrong in their lives that they are forced to look inward. As Kubie[8] has so aptly stated, "There is one instrument which every discipline uses without checking its errors, tacitly assuming that the instrument is error-free. This, of course, is the human psychological apparatus."

Definition of Projective Counseling

In the development of this "new" technique, projective counseling, our major concern has been with prevention rather than cure, with ways of giving psychological insight to those as yet not seriously incapacitated emotionally. As a method it may be described as a re-educational or remedial technique which can be used with individuals, or with couples and groups, and, in essence, it amounts to confronting the person, or persons, with his own productions—with the raw material from the projective tests at those times in the re-educational process when this material can best be

3

used with insight. In this chapter we have chosen brief examples of the use of this technique with one individual, with a small group, and with couples involved in marital problems.

Comparable Techniques

Although we have spoken of this as a new technique, references in the literature can be found to the use of single projective tests in a comparable way. Bellak, Pasquarelli and Braverman[1] have found that T. A. T. material could be used for interpretations to the patient and, further, as associative material in itself. These authors employed it to particular advantage "in cases where there is general blocking, dearth of associations, resistance of any kind, protectiveness, and depression with little verbalization." George Devereaux[2] has used something very comparable in an analysis of the Figure Drawings with a patient. In his account he gives a verbatim report of the interchange between patient and therapist, in this connection the patient moving rapidly to the point where he can accept his drawings as symbolizing some of his key problems.

Since the first publication of this technique,[5] discussion with psychodiagnosticians has shown that, without formalizing or recording their procedure, they have in retrospect seen themselves as employing it. Miale[9] reports on a patient with whom she was working who had reached an impasse and was unable to recognize or accept her major conflicts. Two of her own responses in the Sentence Completion test, responses epitomizing the antagonistic or competing attitudes which she had, were presented to her. At this point she was suddenly able not only to accept this as her own problem but to come to grips with it in a productive way.

Munroe[10] found herself using this method with a group of students with "almost too much success," since even carefully selected items from the tests tended to liberate or trigger too much material for her to handle in the brief session subsequent to the testing procedures which was available for counseling.

Roman—whose *Interaction Testing* appears in this volume— has utilized this technique, subsequent to its formulation, in some experimental work with psychotherapy of *groups* rather than of individuals in a group. By asking persons in a group to produce a joint or group test protocol based on discussion of responses, and then confronting the group with their process and products, he has found that significant insights have been promoted and marked changes in group functioning have taken place. This has been explored in such diverse groups as marriages, delinquent gangs, and groups of psychiatric residents in training.

A Case Example

The case chosen as an example of the individual use of this technique is that of a girl in her early twenties who was seen for intensive counseling sessions over a nine-week period.[4] At the time of referral the outlook was anything but favorable. She was an adopted child, and against a background of difficulties with her parents extending over many years, an immediate crisis had arisen. She had been expelled from her college dormitory, was supposed to have been hopelessly snarled in bad company, associating particularly with—and this is important in the light of the history—a near-blind musician who was with a band known to be using "dope." The patient, herself, was also suspected of taking drugs, although this subsequently proved to be untrue. It was true, however, that she was lying flagrantly in an attempt to ward off her parents' knowledge that she had lost the part-time job necessary for keeping her in college.

While some of the accusations by over-anxious parents and distressed college officials turned out to be exaggerations, it was true that she was completely unable to arouse herself in the morning, would appear "doped," and would have to be dragged out of bed by physical force before she could start the day. Moreover, this inertia carried over into her daily occupation so that she became actually unable to hold her part-time job. A vicious cycle was thus set up whereby she lied and was then afraid to apply for any job.

Despite the fact that her parents considered her to be of mediocre intelligence and treated her as such, the Wechsler-Bellevue indicated an I. Q. of 138. Moreover, the Rorschach, the Figure

Drawing, the Sentence Completion and the Most Unpleasant Concept Test all provided rich material for direct use in projective counseling. There was no question of an underlying psychosis; although a free flow of associative material was maintained, she was never engulfed by uncontrollable moods or fantasies. In terms of attacking the problem with as much dispatch as possible, one aspect of the Szondi was the most arresting and suggestive. This was the 6 -s responses which this patient gave, and which provided a clue to the central immobilizing tendencies and their probable dynamics. It was clear that release of this rigidly repressed aggression must take place before any movement could be expected.

Free associations to the selected answers from the Rorschach almost at once activated memories that converged upon the central theme; namely, her hatred, fear and fascination of her father. A highly significant answer was "a long-nosed wolf." Although not apparent to the patient at first, and followed by evasive associations, this key clue ultimately brought the patient to the consideration of her father's nose (and the whole problem of his being a Jew), of his angry, "animal, wolf-like expression" and from here to the key source of her terror—her father's angry eyes. Her own inability to retaliate in the face of his anger had, to use her own words, "driven her underground." She smoldered but never dared to retaliate. Once, associating to a Sentence Completion and contemplating retaliation, she envisaged herself plunging a pair of scissors into her father and killing him.

Associations to the "eyes" which she had seen in the Rorschach brought this patient quickly to fascinating material. More than anything else, it was "those blazing eyes" which had terrified her. From this she came to understand that her present attachment to an individual who was virtually blind was closely related to the original fear of the penetrating, all-seeing eyes of her father. It was necessary, and safe, to love only some one who could not see. From this it was but a small therapeutic step to a discussion of her inability to open her eyes, and her attempt to shut out the world through continued sleep.

Alternately terrified and attracted by her father, she came close to Oedipal material when free-associating to her drawings. She had drawn the man without a face but with a stick and commented, "I wish he would actually hit me rather than hitting me verbally." In this particular case, no further probing or suggestions were given along these lines since the patient's adjustment in terms of her everyday life was so spectacular that deeper material was not touched on.

The interrelation of the material from the Sentence Completion and Most Unpleasant Concept was used to attack an obviously phobic area for this patient, namely, the "spider." On the Most Unpleasant Concept test a "spider" had been drawn, and several of the sentences in the Holsopple-Miale Sentence Completion showed her concern: "She couldn't bear to touch . . . . the spider," and again, "Closer and closer there comes . . . . a big spider." While the first completion is not unusual, the second alerts one to the pathological aspects of this idea for the patient. The "spider," when she associated to it, led her back along a direct path to the point at which, terrified and yet fascinated by her father, she had gathered spiders to burn them in effigy, believing thereby she could destroy him. Then, terrified by her own daring and cruelty, she would swing to the other extreme and attempt to keep a spider in view at night in a web outside her window. Her profound feelings of hatred of her father, with their ambivalent aspects, were again made known and became at this point an all-important step in her capacity to adjust more realistically to the family situation.

Over a period of several years, now, the therapist has had frequent opportunity to check on her current adjustment. The referring physician, who had known the patient since childhood, made the following summary of her condition:

> A young woman who was adopted by temperamental parents has had all of her relationships contaminated by displaced fears and hostilities. She lived perpetually in a sit-down strike in work and in play, and was bent on destroying herself and punishing her parents by a series of unsuitable alliances and perpetual maladjusted behavior.
>
> This patient during therapy reversed herself completely, came out of her shell, went through normal, transient emotions

of anger which she could correct, and was finally able to make an excellent marriage to an appropriate and healthy young man.

A follow-up two years later indicates continued growth, maturity and adjustment (4).

Group Counseling Sessions

In addition to using projective counseling with individual patients it has been used in small groups. The group counseling sessions which will be described were held at the request of students who took part in a diagnostic and counseling experiment. At the beginning of the freshman year a full battery of psychological tests was administered both to medical students and to students who planned to embark subsequently on intensive training for work in the ministry. A student was entitled to counseling on the basis of his test findings as part of the experimental program. This counseling could be carried on either with the individual alone, or in a group session, which could result in a transfer to more extensive psychotherapy if the occasion warranted.

These group counseling sessions consisted of five or six students. Such a session might start by some one offering a specific problem he was having in regard to academic work. In the session presently considered, Rex told of the problem he was having in understanding the instruction given him by various professors. As a matter of fact, his first formulation ran more in the manner of: "Professors A, B and C are very difficult people to understand; they are confusing in the way they present the material."

With the consent of Rex, the counselor turned to a large chart of the Wechsler-Bellevue scattergram and marked up the scores he had achieved when he had taken the test battery. Rex's scattergram illustrated a sharp drop on the Comprehension score. The meaning of the various subtests and what they attempted to measure was then explained to the group as a whole, and all had evidence of the fact that in the area of general understanding Rex was weak in an absolute sense, and relatively weak when this score was compared to his other achievements. One of the students then commented: "Maybe it isn't the professors who are so difficult to understand after all," and laughed, whereupon Rex became somewhat defensive and turned for corroboration of his original statement to the student beside him.

At this stage the counselor picked up with a slight change of direction asking the group as a whole: "How did most of you answer the question which ran, 'If you are lost in a forest in the daytime how would you find your way out?'" Various "obvious" answers were given but Rex said, still with a considerable degree of conviction, "If I were lost in a forest it would be because some guy had swiped my compass. I always go around with one in my pocket when I'm camping." Bob from the other end of the table replied, "Oh, *his* fault, eh?" and the group laughed. The counselor intervened: "How did most of you answer the question, 'Why is it that persons who are born deaf cannot speak?'" This time Rex piped up first, "It's probably congenital. It's probably the fault of the mother." Here he was playing it both ways, half laughing but still somewhat defensive. He was ready to let the group accept this as a joke, yet this was actually what he had given as his answer when the test had been administered to him.

Another student took up the thread: "Did Rex get a low score on this test because he blamed people other than himself? I don't see what that's got to do with not understanding something. Why does this test measure understanding or 'comprehension,' as you call it? What's getting measured is the fact that old Rex doesn't want to take the responsibility for his own actions." Andrew began hesitantly, "Well if you always think . . . that is . . . if you went around all the time with a pre-established connection in your mind . . . that is . . . if you did, and I'm not saying Rex does, but *if* you did, then you wouldn't see things as they really are, would you? And isn't understanding, seeing things as they are?" This statement was then discussed by the group at considerable length and Andrew was encouraged to amplify his ideas.

Rex now rejoined the discussion and, although he had found the preceding remarks a little disturbing, he wished to be an active participant again: "Supposing some guy gets every single one of these right, what would his answers be? Suppose he does understand perfectly?" The counselor then read off the standard answers and turned the discussion to a consideration of their neutrality, their objectivity, their lack of personal bias. She followed this with examples of different kinds of wrong answers illustrating, or maybe caricaturing, different problems as they are reflected in this test. At this point each student wished to be reminded of the answer he had given when he previously took the test, and set about to assess and detect his own particular biases.

Normative Aspects of Projective Counseling

Another facet of projective counseling which can also take place individually or in groups relates to the use of the more formal aspects of the test findings. This involves placing the individual within a framework derived from the test scores of his peers which is then used as a start towards greater understanding of his own actions, assets and liabilities as related to the group within which he lives. Figure 1 is a chart of a student population in terms of human movement and color responses on the Rorschach. These two factors are explained very generally to the group or the individual student, and illustrations are given as to the personality characteristic of hypothetical individuals located in various positions on the chart. Code numbers are always used, and no student can ever know the position of another member of the group.

Students whom we have called Mr. X and Mr. M., respectively, were shown their positions on the chart to clarify certain aspects of the problems they brought to the counseling session. For example, "X" wanted to find out whether he was really fitted for a given career because, as it seemed to him, his vocation had to compete with so many other interests. To any outsider, this was an obviously gifted boy. Nevertheless, he felt inferior because he could not muster up a single-minded dedication to his chosen field, a dedication which he found highly laudable in others. "X," as it turned out, was quite a gifted poet, sketched and painted on his vacations, and ran through a host of other competing delights. He told of this, however, in a rather self-deprecatory manner.

Locating "X" on the chart finds him as objectively atypical as he himself describes. He was astonished and relieved to have these disturbing hunches crystallized through the test media. The

RORSCHACH INTROVERSION-EXTROVERSION RATIOS EXPRESSED GRAPHICALLY

EXTROVERSION SCORES

C Responses

M Responses	0.	.5	1	1.5	2	2.5	3	3.5	4	4.5	5	5.5	6	6.5	7	7.5
0	151, 128			29	157	149										
1	130, 159, 71	156, 57	72, 59	82	64, 114, 158, 115	152, 103, 92	39		139				129			
2	136, 102, 120, 55, 145, 150, 37	3, 160, 143	41, 121, 93	15, 95, 7, 35	73, 70	68, 125, 113	104, 101	124		54	91					
3	141, 107, 88, 142	6	97, 161, 117, 56, 62, 38, 75, 99, 77, 67	108, 42, 135, 53	46, 61, 19	18	40, 153, 144	12, 60A		111						11
4	85, 27	133, 69, 123, 22	58, 146, 48, 50	78, 106, 134, 105	20, 21, 52, 118, 31, 109, 87	1, 110	14, 31A	47	79, 25							
5	45	36, 148, 44	60, 51, 122, 28, 132, 4	155, 154, 147	26	140, 131, 127	76, 16									
6	8, 83	63, 18A, 116, 5, 33, 81	32, 86	90, 100	126, 43, 84		23				119					
7	105A	74	96, 138		137	30		80			24	17				Mr. X
8					65	98										
9		49		89, 50A			9	10	2							
10-11			Mr. M.				34, 13, 66									
14																

INTROVERSION SCORES

Fig. 1

counselor's task from here on was to discuss the assets and liabilities of being out in this artistic, intellectual left field, and to clarify the importance of incorporating, rather than renouncing, these rather unusual interests and assets. When "X" was seen three years later he had had no academic difficulty and was progressing well. The brief counseling session seems to have been an important one in that it freed him from the totally unnecessary feelings of guilt as to his own usefulness.*

Another comparable case, located in a different part of the extroversion-introversion map, was the would-be minister whose ascetic appearance resulted in his description as the "mystic" (Mr. M.). This individual falls off the chart with 14 M responses to 1 color response and comes to the counseling session with the rather understandable complaint that he doesn't know how he is going to make the grade in his work with his congregation. Scholastically he is doing extraordinarily well, but he claims he is ecstatically happy only when spending hours reading and speculating philosophically.

Again, this student found considerable relief in *locating* himself on a map with reference to others, and again the session hinged around the inevitable difficulties inherent in one who held such an atypical position in the total population.* Such discussions clearly do not bring about a basic personality change. Nonetheless, they have seemed many times to give the individual a perspective of his assets and liabilities so that he plans with greater insight for their best usage.

---

* On graduating, four years later, X wrote:

"To refresh your memory, I was one of the guinea pigs in the freshman psychological testing program conducted here in the fall of 1954. On your graphs, etc., you located me in the extremity in a rather isolated fashion and made several prognostications about my forthcoming years in medical school.

"I simply wanted you to know it was interesting to note much of what you said has proved to be true, but despite the system I will graduate.

"Your work has always been keenly interesting to me, and again I would like to thank you for your time with us."

* A followup of this student four years later showed that he had abandoned the idea of active church work, and had entered the field of advanced scholarship.

Projective Counseling with Marriage Partners

A third field where this technique has proved of value has been in marriage counseling. This involves joint sessions with couples involved in marital difficulties, or with engaged couples who hesitate to take the final step. Such counseling does not concern itself only with the insights which can be derived from the test findings of the individuals involved. Rather an attempt is made to clarify areas of potential difficulties which may arise between persons differently endowed psychologically. In locating a person's score, the counselor is always careful to point up that *any* position on the test chart has advantages as well as disadvantages and there is no constellation of traits which cannot be used to advantage for both personal and interpersonal satisfaction. However, the difficulties which are likely to beset some types of individuals in their interactions with others are discussed.

It is interesting to note that W. Grey Walter[12] has developed a comparable type of marital counseling on the basis of EEG records. Walter states that the actual functioning of the brain may be shown to differ in two individuals with correspondingly different ways of reacting to, and assessing, everyday situations. "Fortunately," he states, "extreme types are rare; but when two people display unreasonable and irreconcilable differences of approach to a question, before concluding that this is due to innate antagonism or incompatibility of purpose, a discrepancy in their ways of thinking may be worth looking into." And for Walter, "ways of thinking" are the direct counterpart of the different brainwaves which the EEG shows.

Understanding of a different "way of looking at the world" can be well presented in projective counseling through the study of a single Rorschach card by both partners simultaneously. Many times one member of the pair will show a holistic approach; the other a much more detailed one. It is then possible to assess the holistic approach both in terms of its achievement as an integrated process and as a potential liability in the tendency of such persons to gloss over important aspects of a problem. Similarly, the more pedantic, literal, and detailed orientation can be seen advantageously in terms of its accuracy, yet at the same time its limitations can be noted. No special training is needed for the average individual to understand this, or to be startled by the realization that the "obvious" things of his own perception are not necessarily the "obvious" objects for some one else. It is not a far cry from this perceptual realization to the understanding that the differences in ideas and concepts may arise from different ways of envisaging the world. The common denominator in many such counseling sessions, in this test and in others, seems to be the removal of the threat that there is implied hostility in the partner's different experiences. The tangible test scores somehow bring reassurance and an understanding of the fact that "this is the way the partner is." This replaces the feeling that differences are somehow a way of showing a critical approach.

The Wechsler-Bellevue scattergrams can also be used in a comparable way to demonstrate patterns of assets and liabilities to the partners. An important stage was reached in the regular psychotherapeutic treatment of Mrs. Z, for instance, when a joint counseling session was held with her and her husband after he had also consented to take the test battery. At this time their contrasting scores convinced him that it was, to a large measure, his insistence on an intellectual perfectionism that was contributing to the anxiety and feeling of insecurity in his wife.

Strangely enough, although the detailed implications of the Szondi test cannot be understood by the layman, it has proved one of the most effective means of bringing understanding and mutual respect for different modes of emotional reactivity. The discussion of different patterns, whereby the psychophysical organism works through and out of pressures and tensions, makes it possible for one member of the pair to envisage the partner's emotional outbursts with a neutrality which makes them much less threatening. In discussing the Szondi from a hypothetical profile, it is possible to convey easily the difference between a loaded vector and an open and discharging one and, with these concepts established, the discussion can proceed. Patients themselves, as a matter of fact, quickly give their own explanations in non-technical terms. As Mrs. R. said, pointing to the high "$+e$" column, "'Oh, that's the pressure in my control box and it's rising to the point where it will blow the lid off and that," pointing to the open "e" and open "hy" of her husband's profile, "that's the leaky tap— that's his anger always dripping but never spurting or gushing."

In a study of forty couples with marital difficulties (some aspects of which have been reported elsewhere[6]) it was found that over 30 per cent showed Szondi scores with the paroxysmal vector of loaded "+e" and loaded "—hy" for one partner, and open "e," "—hy," or "—e" and "—hy" for another. Invariably, in these cases, each partner was preoccupied with the other's emotional difficulties and the descriptions were of two kinds: "He (or she) has, on occasion, violent hysterical outbursts" countered with, "She (or he) often snaps my head off but the very next moment doesn't seem to remember that she (or he) has been angry." The former description, of course, belongs to those individuals who push control to a point where there is a sudden and violent breakdown; the latter, to those whose mode of discharging tension follows a series of minor, tension-releasing episodes.

A Summary Chart similar to that shown in Figure 2 can be used advantageously in counseling in several ways.[3] The respective positions of the two partners in regard to the various categories can be discussed jointly in detail. Figure 2 contrasts the findings of a husband and wife, where the circle indicates the wife's performance and the square that of the husband. It will be seen that the wife is less intelligent, in terms of formal testing, but more productive and original; also more anxious. The assets, liabilities and difficulties of these individuals in their attempted interaction as marital partners can be well illustrated by these test findings.

In cases where the patient's test performance in many areas is far superior to his self-concept, it can form an authoritative background with very reassuring aspects. Individuals are often asked to react to this assessment of themselves, and the discrepancies of their own estimation and the test findings can be utilized for further discussion.

Organization in Perception and Behavior

How the individual uses the space which is allotted to him for the completion of a task, and the implications from this as to how

SUMMARY OF TEST FINDINGS

MANNER DURING TEST

(1) Overly distressed	(2) Tense	(3) Indifferent	(4) Appropriate	(5) Relaxed and actively interested
(1) Hostile	(2) Uneasy			

I.Q. (Bellevue-Wechsler)

(1) Below average	(2) Average	(3) High average	(4) Superior	(5) Very superior

PRODUCTIVITY (Rorschach)

(1) Impoverished	(2) Reduced output	(3) Adequate	(4) Better than average	(5) Rich and well-ordered
	(2) Compulsive productivity			

RELATION TO REALITY (Rorschach, Bellevue-Wechsler, Drawings)

(1) Loose	(2) Lapses—together with good form	(3) Not noticeably disturbed	(4) Essentially firm	(5) Firm and good

USUAL-UNUSUAL THOUGHT CONTENT (Rorschach, Unpleasant Concept)

(1) Bizarre	(2) Tendency toward the bizarre	(3) Adequate	(4) Original trends	(5) Outstandingly original
(1) Stereotyped	(2) Tendency toward stereotypy			

CONSTRUCTIVE FANTASY (Rorschach)

(1) Absent	(2) Barely accessible	(3) Accessible	(4) Readily accessible	(5) Active but not hampering
(1) Withdrawal into fantasy				

DRIVE (Rorschach, Szondi, Unpleasant Concept)

(1) Overpowering aggression	(2) Over-aggressive	(3) Adequate	(4) Clearly sufficient	(5) Sufficient— exceptionally well-directed
(1) Hampering passivity	(2) Insufficient drive			

EMOTIONAL TONE (Rorschach, Szondi)

(1) Explosive emotions	(2) Getting out of hand	(3) Trend toward emotional expression	(4) Warmth available	(5) Warm, readily available
(1) Lacking	(2) Indicated but repressed emotions			

SOCIAL ATTITUDE (T. A. T.)

(1) Uncontrolled	(2) Constricted or neglected	(3) Adequate	(4) Well-regulated	(5) Free and flexible

ANXIETY

(1) Disintegrating	(2) Marked	(3) Moderate	(4) Not marked	(5) Lack of evidence of anxiety

OVER-ALL EVALUATION

(1) Markedly disturbed personality	(2) Less than adequate personality with some psychological problems	(3) Adequate personality	(4) Better than average functioning personality	(5) Exceptionally well-integrated personality with excellent potential

Fig. 2

he uses his "life space," has long interested graphologists and psychologists concerned with graphic productions such as Figure Drawings and the House-Tree-Person.

For several years now we have been using expendable editions of the Harrower Inkblots with instructions to the subject to write his responses directly on the white space around the blot itself, and as part of his immediate task, to indicate the whereabouts of these responses. Details of this method are found elsewhere.[7]

As may well be expected, an enormous variation occurs from individual to individual while following out the identical instructions, and it is possible to make an assessment not only on the Rorschach responses in the usual manner but to subject the writing to graphological analysis with particular emphasis on the use of the allotted space and the handling of the locating of the responses.

"Blind analysis" by several graphologists on the basis of such material alone corresponded very closely to psychodiagnostic appraisals which were drawn from a full battery of tests including the Rorschach proper. For in the words of one of our graphological colleagues taking part in this experiment, "The grouping of words, their clustering or dispersion, the distance between the written test and the blots to which they refer, are most characteristic and provide entirely new facets for the interpretation of the use of space."

What we are concerned with here, however, is *the use of a patient's own productions in a counseling session* to illustrate some problem which is under consideration therapeutically. This is done at the appropriate time by allowing the patient to review his own raw material in the inkblot series as a whole, or to compare his performance on one specific card with that of some other person.

Subject A, for instance, gained insight through this method into her unwillingness to become involved, her need for distance and remoteness, with its concomitant trend to self-protective frigidity, when comparing her productions with the energetic, and as she described it, "vehement involvement" in the task at hand of Subject B who was following the same instructions and treating the same card.

Again, Subject C, when first tested prior to counseling sessions, was so overpowered by his wealth of imagery that this phase of the test—namely, to record his responses in an allotted space—was well nigh impossible for him. Much of his therapeutic progress was represented by his gaining increasing control, in learning to organize, rather than be engulfed by, his flow of associations. The example which is given here comes at a stage of counseling where he became aware, explicitly for the first time, of the conflict of the richness of his productions and the need for order. Moreover, contrasting his responses to Card VIII with that of a comparable attempt by a completely impoverished subject (Subject D), he realized the assets as well as the liabilities of his fertile mind. Figures 3, 4, 5 and 6 represent the productions of Subjects A, B, C and D respectively.

Other types of comparisons can be made in the same way, for example the scattered and somewhat disorganized handiwork of Subject E on Harrower blot 1 (Figure 7) can be contrasted with the compulsively methodical work of Subject F on Harrower blot X (Figure 8). The free hand and artistic embellishment of his response on Card V turned sidewards (Figure 9) given by Subject G can be contrasted with the very literal rendition of the instructions by Subject H, whose work is illustrated by his handling of Card VI (Figure 10). The expansive and verbal production of Subject J, seen on Harrower Card IV (Figure 11) can be compared with the need to provide a protective circle for each of his responses, as shown in the work of Subject K on Card II (Figure 12).

Although not necessarily used in counseling sessions, it may be worthwhile to round out the ten-card series by showing different types of response locating patterns for cards III, VII and IX respectively. Here we find on Card III an unusual tendency to "frame" a response with a uniform white margin, and on cards VII and IX examples of left and right marginal clinging (Figures 13, 14, 15). For those unfamiliar with this inkblot series it should be stated that, while reproduced here in black and white only, the

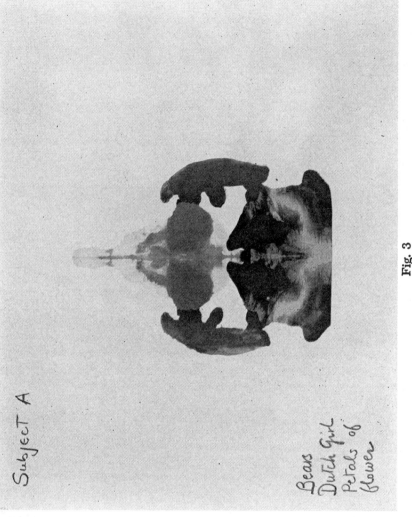

Fig. 3

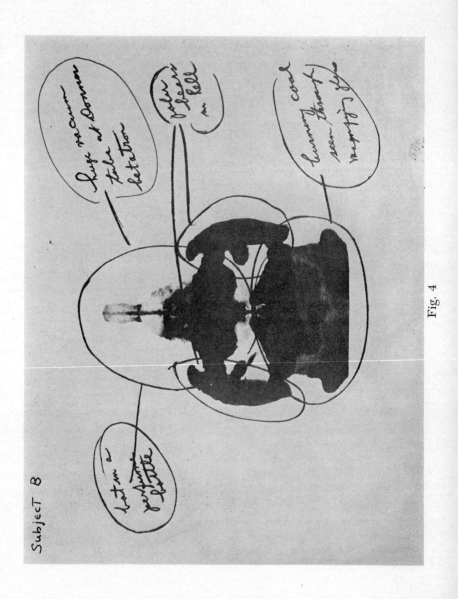

Fig. 4

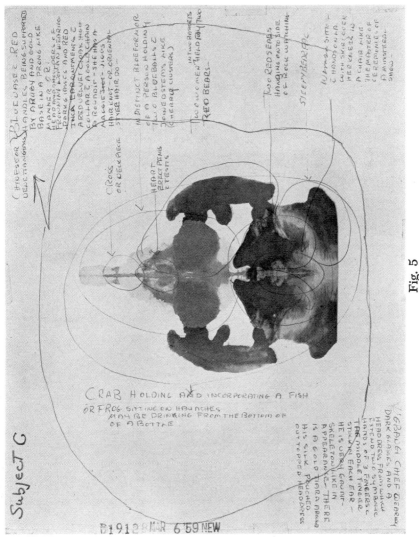

Fig. 5

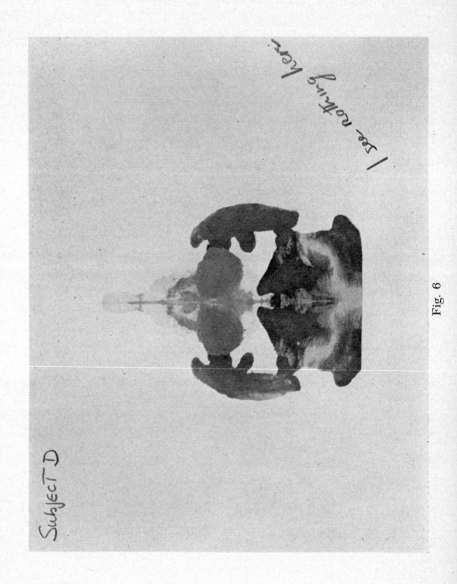

Fig. 6

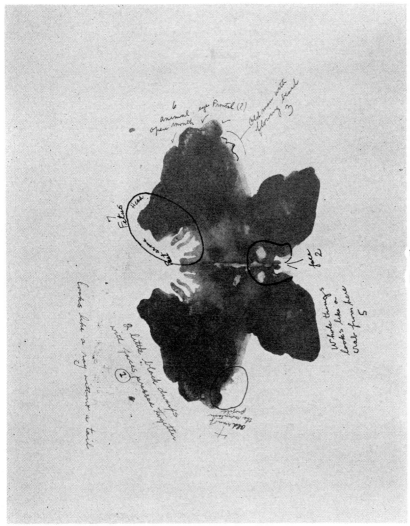

Fig. 7

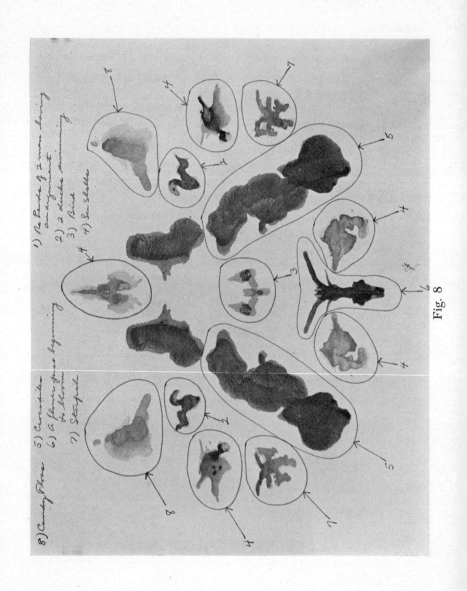

Fig. 8

Fig. 9

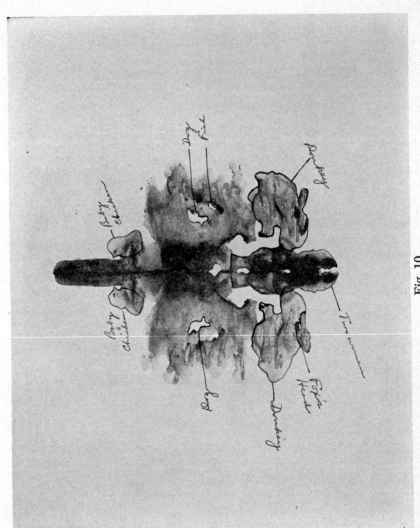

Fig. 10

Fig. 11

Fig. 12

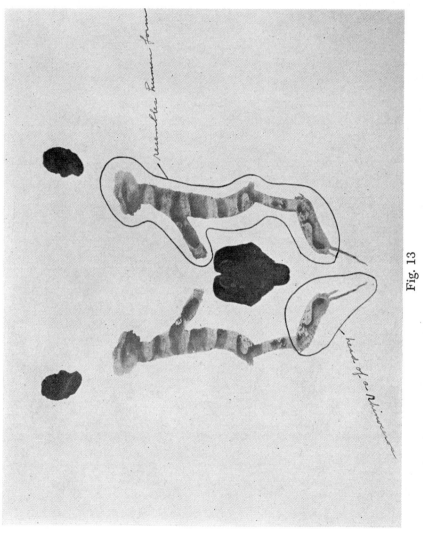

Fig. 13

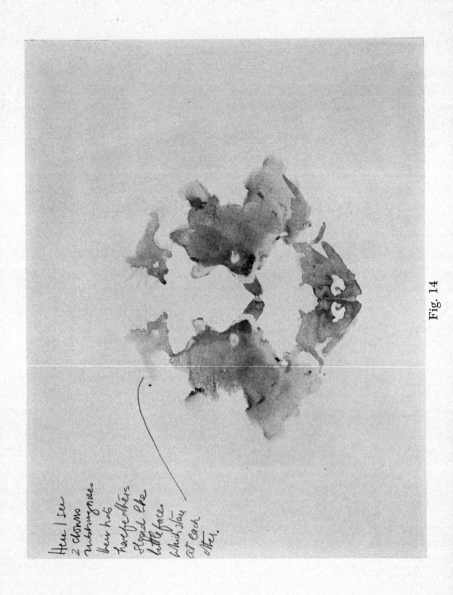

Fig. 14

Fig. 15

originals include two black, white and red cards (II and III) and three full colored cards (VIII, IX, X).

When these inkblots are used in counseling sessions the patient or subject is given the opportunity to get insights into his own work habits by describing the differences between his own productions and that of others. The counselor is not interested in praise or blame, in making one type of production appear better than another. The object is rather to provide an opportunity for perspective, perspective in the sense that an attitude or activity previously taken for granted as "the only way to respond to instructions" may have highly idiosyncratic components in it.

Contrasting Rational and Projective Material

On some occasions we have confronted an individual with *two aspects of his own productions*—his rational opinion as expressed in a questionnaire, on the one hand, and some of his projective material, on the other. The comparison has allowed the subject to question the complete "objectivity" of his opinions, and has opened the door to further insights as to his own motivations.

For example, in a testing and counseling program of thirty foremen in an industrial concern, a questionnaire revealed that Foreman Y was unwilling to allow greater freedom in working arrangements to his subordinates. On discussion he backed up his opinion in the questionnaire on purely rational grounds in terms of the advantages of his close supervision for the benefit of the company.

His projective material, however, revealed his own excessive need to overprotect and nurture those who were working under him. This was strikingly shown in a modification of the draw-a-person test where two people, a foreman and a worker, must be portrayed. In response to these instructions Foreman Y had drawn a picture of a mother with a large family of children seated at a table getting food, labeling the mother as the foreman and the children as the workers! Free associating to this, and discussing the implications of his drawing gave him insight into his own personal needs—his overprotectiveness and oversolicitousness. He was then able to withdraw his violent objection to the suggestions that were being made, concerning greater opportunities for freedom among his subordinates, and could relinquish such vigilant control over their activities.

Direct vs Indirect Use of Projective Material

We have made the distinction elsewhere of the direct, as opposed to the indirect, use of projective material.[4] By direct use is meant the sharing of responses with the patient to allow further reactions to them, or to use them as a basis for interpretation of attitudes and feelings. By indirect use is meant the continued and up-to-date briefing of the counselor of immediate pressures, or of new conflicts which may be detected from the tests but which are not necessarily brought into the therapeutic hour by the patient, or commented on by the counselor. Some of the projective tests may be repeated at each session more easily than others and a "house," drawn and described has proved a useful one.

The houses drawn by Mrs. R., for instance, were used at one stage to show her her own progress and movement in treatment, a fact which she was loath to accept. It became clear during an early session that the house she drew symbolized herself. Her first attempt, drawn in her initially depressed, self-castigation period, was described by her as a "barren, empty little hut. It doesn't even have windows; they're all boarded up." This not only describes her own feelings of being barren and worthless but the hopelessness of the non-existent outlook for the future. After five drawings taken a week apart, and each showing a slightly more attractive building, she drew her first "house with a view." The sequence of houses was then discussed with her and she spontaneously accepted that the outlook from the house was now her changed point of view, and even suggested that perhaps the more pleasant looking structure was herself, i.e., the place she was "looking out from." At this point she began to be less self-critical, accepting her own "indirect" assessment of herself more readily.

Questions Frequently Asked

It may be of interest at this point to raise some of the questions which are asked of those who use projective counseling, and to give some brief answers to them.

1. What criteria are used for accepting or rejecting patients for projective counseling?

If a patient's projective material is to be used as a basis for giving insight, it must meet certain requirements: First, it must be sufficiently "rich" so that use can be made of it in many areas. The completely impoverished Rorschach record cannot be used advantageously. Second, the individual must show sufficient ego-strength and adequate controls so as to be able to handle anxieties which may be mobilized. Third, since much of this method rests on the completely frank sharing of material between counselor and patient, we have considered it unwise to use this method with individuals whose position on the various formal charts appears precarious. Where the individual is unaware of his own potentials, or envisages himself as much more of an inadequate person than he actually is, this method is particularly valuable. Miale goes so far as to state that she finds it of great use "in convincing some individuals that they do *not* need psychotherapy"!

2. Is a diagnosis made before projective counseling begins?

Diagnosis in the formal, psychiatric sense is less important here than a very careful study of the total record derived from the battery of six or seven projective techniques. Thus, a diagnosis is made as to whether or not this individual can be reasonably expected to profit from this technique. It is also essential to be fully aware of those areas which are most apt to precipitate one into the handling of major conflicts and, conversely, to be aware of the patient's achievements or assets. Munroe[11] speaks of "tailoring therapy" to fit the patient's special needs. The detailed projective assessment, as opposed to the mere psychiatric classification, which is possible from projective tests, allows of differentiation within any psychiatric group. Two classifiable hysterics, for instance, may nonetheless show enormously different personality patterns within this general grouping. Diagnosis in this added sense is very important.

3. *Are attempts made to persuade the patient to change his environment?*

"Persuade" is too strong a word. One would not hesitate to reinforce tentative suggestions made by the patient as to possible environmental changes, and would utilize material from the projective techniques to convince him that he or she had sufficient strength to carry out a change that he was contemplating. Mrs. T., for instance, was reassured by a consideration of the pattern which she showed on the Summary Chart, that she was strong enough to step into an essentially therapeutic role in her marriage, a role of holding down the fort, for a time, while her husband obtained intensive treatment. In so doing she went through with various necessary changes in terms of their living arrangements, etc., which she probably would not have done otherwise.

4. *How is the projective counselor's role conceptualized?*

In projective counseling the therapist *shares* material with the patient which is of interest to both of them because it throws light on the patient's difficulties. Where disturbances and inadequacies show up in the test findings, the therapist does not minimize them or cushion them but assumes that these difficulties will be tackled and handled in a kind of partnership. In a way, both therapist and patient look to the projective material for insights which can be gained from its understanding.

5. *Is there a theory behind projective counseling?*

Projective counseling is not so much a theory as a technique which, in a special way, allows the individual to come to grips with some of his own problems by gaining perspective on his test productions within a wider framework. Perhaps the most striking common denominator of all cases counseled in this way is the relief and reassurance that can be given to the patient by means of *some tangible, conceptual model, providing him with some way of coming to grips intellectualy with a chaos of confused feelings.* Inadequate as their understanding of a Szondi profile may be, from a technical point of view, nonetheless for Mr. and Mrs. X. it provided a *working model* which helped them deal with important emotional experiences. It is a common finding in projective counseling that patients reiterate the relief from anxiety which they have, following their being able to employ these working models, and in describing their feelings more accurately.

6. *Do patients develop sufficient insight to maintain improvement?*

The individual case discussed in detail unquestionably developed sufficient insight to *handle the immediate problem* and extricate herself from the vortex of confusion into which she was rapidly spiraling. Insight into many related problems was not attempted, and a five-year followup indicates that there are still unsolved problems which would benefit by more extensive psychological help. Many of the couples who have unquestionably benefited by projective counseling have said, in the words of Mrs. J., "Some of the ideas we got from you at that time have gone on working somewhere inside me ever since. I thought of calling you recently when Y (her daughter) was having some difficulties in school but remembered our discussion of those women in the inkblots who looked as if they were 'shouting at somebody' and I began to see what I, myself, was doing to precipitate some of Y's difficulties."

7. *If one considers a continuum to exist from superficial to deep psychotherapy, where would projective counseling be placed?*

Basically projective counseling remains on a relatively superficial level. What happens frequently, however, is that subsequent to handling of specific crises and problems by this means, the individual decides to go into deeper treatment.

8. *How is projective counseling terminated?*

This type of counseling is usually terminated when the patient feels he or she has derived the maximum benefit from the sessions, or when the presenting problem has ceased to be acute, or when all the material in the projectives that can yield insight has been exhausted and a stable plateau of adjustment seems to have been reached.

Conclusions

In concluding this chapter, the following points may be emphasized: First, it is clear that there is no one correct way of using any of the projective tests, nor is there a prescribed sequence, nor need all tests used for diagnostic purposes be employed therapeutically.

Second, in order to use this technique effectively the therapist must become steeped in the patient's productions. Not only must the material have been thoroughly assessed, but most of the nuances must have been learned so that any aspect is available to be "played back" to the patient at the appropriate time.

Third, it should not be thought that this is a technique which absorbs the counseling session exclusively. It cannot be divorced from other approaches, and cannot take place until an initial feeling of trust for the therapist has been established with the patient. As Munroe has stated so well, "No formal device can substitute for the feeling of being understood and accepted."[11] It is often necessary, in initial interviews with projective counseling, to convey one's capacity for understanding swiftly and strikingly by utilizing some information from the raw data of the patient's test protocol in the very first session. Thus Mrs. B., who could not draw well but whose total record gave evidence of great sensitivity and creativeness, was startled and immediately anchored in the technique by the comment, "You are obviously very artistic. Are you finding some outlet for this at the present time?" Mrs. B., who was indeed a gifted painter and interior decorator but knew this to be unknown to the therapist at the time, overcame much of her initial hesitation as a result of the fact that her "artistic" nature could actually be known from the test despite her poor drawings. To use Munroe's terms, the counselor in this instance had also "made the grade."

One final word of caution: The possible dangers of the use of this technique by unqualified persons have, of course, been given consideration. The crux of the matter lies in what constitutes "qualifications." All psychotherapeutic techniques can be abused, and projective counseling is certainly no exception. Thus, the mere formulation of "dos" and "don'ts" will not protect the method from misuse. Perhaps the major safeguard that can be formulated at this time is the strong recommendation that it be employed only by *trained* therapists who, at the same time, have ample experience with projective tests.

The first requirement is the important one, namely, the thorough therapeutic training, for it is very unlikely that the established therapist unversed in the projectives would be interested in adding this to his own techniques. On the other hand, it may well prove unduly inviting to the psychodiagnosticians *without therapeutic training* who would assume that he was qualified by virtue of his outstanding diagnostic competence.

The therapeutically untrained psychodiagnostician, along with the student of psychodiagnostics, is often unaware of the disruptive anxiety which may be mobilized in a patient when too penetrating illustrations are given from the test material. The eager student, it is well known, has an urge to give interpretations and "insights" from the test material to his "guinea pigs," and this tendency is cautioned against by all seasoned instructors in psychodynamic methods and the proper safeguards are erected. But beyond the student stage, the experienced psychodiagnostician may need the same warning if he is tempted to plunge too quickly into the counseling field by virtue of his diagnostic acumen. Projective counseling should augment therapeutic training but should never be considered as a short-cut method.

Bibliography

1. Bellak, L., Pasquarelli, B. A., and Braverman, S.: The use of the thematic apperception test in psychotherapy. *J. Nerv. & Ment. Dis., 64:* 110, 1949.
2. Devereux, G.: *Reality and Dream: The Psychotherapy of a Plains Indian.* New York; International Press, 1951, pp. 177-184, 194-195, 342-343, 417-420, plates 9 and 10.
3. Harrower, Molly: *Personality Change and Development as Measured by the Projective Techniques.* New York, Grune and Stratton, Inc., 1958.
4. Harrower, Molly: Projective Counseling. A psychotherapeutic technique. *Am. J. Psychotherapy, 10:* 74-86, 1956.

5. Harrower, Molly: Projective Tests and Psychotherapy in Wolff, W. *Contemporary Psychotherapists Examine Themselves.* Springfield, Charles C Thomas, 1956, pp. 184-191.

6. Harrower, Molly: The Measurement of Psychological Factors in Marital Maladjustment in Eisenstein V. W.: *Neurotic Interaction in Marriage.* New York, Basic Books, Inc., 1956, pp. 169-191.

7. Harrower, Molly: *Manual for Self-administered Inkblots.* In preparation.

8. Kubie, L. S.: The forgotten man of education. *Harvard Alumni Bull.,* 8: 349-353, 1954.

9. Miale, F. R.: Personal communication.

10. Munroe, R. L.: Personal communication.

11. Munroe, R. L.: Intellectualizing Techniques in Psychotherapy in *Case Studies of Counseling and Psychotherapy,* to be published, New York, Prentice-Hall, Inc.

12. Walter, W. G.: *The Living Brain.* New York, W. W. Norton and Company, Inc., 1953, pp. 220-222.

THE STRUCTURED INTERVIEW TECHNIQUE

PAULINE G. VORHAUS, Ed.D.*

I. Manual of Administration and Evaluation

A. *Introduction*

THE procedure which comprises The Structured Interview may be summarized as follows:

1. The subject is asked to draw a person. In the unusual instances where the drawing is of the opposite sex, he is then asked to make an own-sex drawing.

2. After he has completed his own-sex drawing, he is asked the series of questions given below concerning the own-sex figure he has drawn. These responses are recorded and numbered on the left side of a vertically folded paper; this being Part I of the Structured Interview.

3. He is then asked the same questions about himself as he was first asked about the figure he had drawn. These responses are recorded and numbered on the right side of the same vertically folded paper; comprising Part II of the Structured Interview.

B. *Structured Interview Questions*

1. Age (How old should we say he is?)
2. Occupation (What shall we say he does?)
3. Education (How far did he get in school?)
4. Type of student (Average — better — less good?)
5. Childhood behavior
    a. Classroom behavior as a child (good — mischievous — bad?)
    b. Home behavior (What was he like at home?)

---

* From the New York Regional Office of the Veterans Administration.

6. Relationship to parents
   a. Is he more like his mother or his father?
   b. In which way?
   c. With which parent did he get along better as a child?
   d. Are both parents still living?
   e. If not, when did the death (or deaths) occur?
   f. If so, with which parent does he get along better, now that he is an adult?)

7. Home attitudes
   a. Strict, moderate, spoiling?
   b. How did he feel about this?
   c. Religious upbringing (strict, moderate, none?)
   d. How did he feel about it?

8. Health
   a. Is he healthy?
   b. If not, what is wrong?
   c. How was his health in childhood?
   d. Were his parents fussy about his health?
   e. If yes, what aspect?
   f. How did he feel about it?

9. Appetite
   a. Now
   b. In childhood?

10. Sleep (Does he sleep well, or des he have difficulty falling asleep?)
    a. Now?
    b. In childhood?
    c. Waking up (does he wake up easily, or have difficulty waking up?)
       (1) Now?
       (2) In childhood?

11. Intelligence
    a. Bright, brighter than average, less bright?)
    b. What was the period of his best functioning?
    c. Why? (What made that a particularly good period?)

12. Memory
    a. Good, better than average, less good than average?
    b. How far back does his memory go?
    c. What is his earliest memory?

13. Disposition? (Calm, calmer than average, less calm than average?)

14. How does he like to spend his time?

15. Popularity
    a. Do people like him?
    b. Was he well liked as a child?
    c. Does he get on better with men or with women?
    d. How about when he was a child?

16. Nature
    a. Happy, happier than average, less happy?
    b. What was the happiest period of his life?
    c. Why? In which way?
    d. What was the hardest period of his life?
    e. Why? In which way?

17. Sociable
    a. Would he rather do the kind of things one does with others or does alone?
    b. If sociable, does he prefer one or two close friends or is he more of a "group person"?
    c. What kind of things does he especially like to do with them?

18. Best things about him?

19. Worst thing?

20. Marital life?
    a. Is he married?
    b. If not—does he look forward to being married some day?
    If married, is it a good marriage (average, better, less good?)
    d. What is particularly good (or bad) about it?
    e. Sexual adjustment (average, better, less good?)

21. Children
    a. Does he have children?
    b. If not, does he look forward to having them some day?
    c. If children, does he, in general, bring them up the way he was brought up or differently?
    d. If no children, when he thinks of having them some day, does he think he will bring them up the way he was brought up, or differently?
    e. If differently, in which way?
22. Wish. (If he could have the proverbial wish, what would it be?)
23. What kind of things make him angry? (Get on his nerves?)
    a. Now?
    b. In childhood?
    c. What does he do when he gets angry?
    d. What did he do as a child?
24. What kind of things put him in a good mood?
    a. Now?
    b. In childhood?
25. What kind of things is he afraid of?
    a. Now?
    b. In childhood?
26. What is his ambition?
    a. Now?
    b. In childhood?
27. Problems
    a. What does he think of as his chief problem?
    b. How does he account for it?
    c. What was his chief problem in childhood?
28. Siblings?
    a. Does he have any brothers or sisters?
    b. Relationship to them?
    c. Relationship in childhood?
    d. Was there a favorite child in the home?
    e. If yes, which?
    f. Favorite of one or both parents?
    g. How did he feel about it?

29. Grandparents
    a. Living?
    b. If not, were they living when he was a child?
    c. If living, present relationship to them?
    d. Childhood relationship to them?
30. If he could change one thing in his life, (live it over) what would it be?
31. Is there anything special that seems worth while to round out the picture?

C. *Administration*

At the outset, it must be emphasized that examiner flexibility is so essential an attribute of this test, and rigidity so against its spirit, that there are no "rules for administration," but merely guideposts. The particular choice of words, as well as inclusion or exclusion of specific questions, and sometimes the order of asking these questions, must vary according to the examiner-client situation. For example, at times questions about childhood experiences may more advantageously precede those relating to adult life; at other times, not.

Part I is presented as follows: "I am now going to give you a test for which you will have to use your imagination. I am going to ask you questions about the make-believe person you drew before (at this point the examiner places the own-sex drawing which the subject has made in the previously administered Draw-A-Person Test** on the table before the subject.) The idea is to pretend that he (or she) is a *real* person, one whom you know well enough to answer questions about. Even if you do not think it is at all a good drawing, that does not matter. I am only using the drawing because most people find it easier to pretend in this way, with a picture before them. So the important thing is to pre-

---

** The writer wants to make acknowledgements to Karen Machover, not only for her Draw-A-Person Test and the list of questions which appear in her book,[1] many of which are repeated here either wholly or in modified form, but also for her explanation of the use of the questions, made in personal communications in the early phases of the development of the Structured Interview.

tend that he (or she) is real, and that you know him (or her) well enough to answer the questions."

Question 1 might then be introduced by saying, "For instance, how old should we say he is?" (It might be added, parenthetically, that the use of the words "should *we* say" has seemed to the writer to facilitate the ease of responding, possibly because it suggests that this is a cooperative enterprise. In those questions which lend themselves to this form, therefore, it is suggested, particularly at first, that the questions be asked in this way. With certain subjects, however, a less personal approach appears preferable. Question 7, for example, might then be worded ("would the home be described as strict, moderate or spoiling?").

In general, the questions are self-explanatory. Questions 18 and 19 however, require an introductory word of explanation. Question 18 is best introduced by the statement: "Everyone has some good things about him, and others that are not so good. In that sense, what would be the *best thing* about him?" Question 19 would then be preceded by the query: "And, in the same sense, what is the *worst thing* about him?" Since no timing is involved, the examiner can feel free to slow the subject up, so as to get a verbatim account.

It frequently happens that, somewhere before the end, the subject announces that he is really speaking about himself. In that event it seems wise to acknowledge that this often happens and to suggest that in spite of this, the test be continued. One might explain: "I'd like to go on with the questions anyhow, if you don't mind, since it often happens that in answer to some of the questions, people prefer to change things, and not describe the situation precisely the way it happened to them. So I'll go on asking questions about the 'person,' and you can do as you like about the way you answer." The next few questions are introduced with the words, "What shall we say about *his* health, or appetite, (or whatever the question related to).

Sometimes people start right off with the announcement, "I am going to talk about myself." In that case the examiner might answer, "Well, you can do as you think about it, but since this is a test of imagination, it would be better if you tried not to stick too closely to your own situation. It may well be that at least in certain questions, you will find that you can use your imagination in this way." Again, the wording of the question would be, "How old should we say he is?" (With a slight stress on the word *he*.)

Occasionally, however, in spite of a willingness to cooperate, it becomes increasingly difficult for the subject to answer the questions with regard to a hypothetical person. In that case, after one or at most two attempts, it seems worth dropping Part I and proceeding with Part II.

Part II is introduced as follows: "There is a second part to this test. This part is called the Same-Different Technique. (This is said to re-emphasize the 'test aspects' of the searching and personal questions.) I am now going to ask you the same questions about yourself that I asked you about the 'make-believe person.' If the answer is the same for you, as it was for him, all you have to do is say, 'same.' If it is different, tell me in which way it is different." For the first few questions, it is important that the examiner quite obviously writes down S (same) or D (different) before writing whatever verbalizations the subject gives. One might encourage such additional verbalizations with the words, "Even if it is the same for you, it may be that you will want to add something—an explanation, or a further statement. Whenever that is so, feel free to add it."

In asking the first few questions, one might say, "You said, for instance, that his age is —. How about *you*; is it the same or different in your case? Or, "you spoke of his occupation as —, what kind of work do *you* do?" After a few questions, this referring back can usually be dropped, to be taken up again whenever the examiner senses that some question is likely to be particularly threatening.

D. *Training of Interpreter*

It seems most appropriate, in considering this question, to quote Murray's words, as given in his manual on the Thematic Apperception Test[2] (substituting the word "Structured Interview responses" for "TAT stories"), "A layman with refined intraceptive intuition and beginner's luck can often, without any experience in testing, make valid and important inferences by feeling his way into the mental environment of the author of a set of TAT stories; and even an old hand at the game must rely on the same process—empathetic intuition first and last, disentangled as far as possible from personal elements. No true scientist will scorn the use of a function which when properly disciplined is capable of yielding precise and pertinent information. Of course intuition alone is highly unreliable; what is required is a rigorously trained, critical intuition.

"Beside a certain flair for the task, the interpreter of the TAT (Structured Interview) should have a background of clinical experience, observing, interviewing and testing patients of all sorts; and, if he is to get much below the surface, knowledge of psychoanalysis and some practice in translating the imagery of dreams and ordinary speech into elementary psychological components. In addition, he should have had months of training in the use of this specific test, much practice in analyzing stories when it is possible to check each conclusion against the known facts of thoroughly studied personalities. Interpretations in vacuo often do more harm than good, since the apparent plausibility of clever interpretations creates convictions which merely serve to confirm the interpreter in the error of his ways. TAT stories (Structured Interview responses) offer boundless opportunities for the projection of one's own complexes or one's pet theories, and the amateur psychoanalyst who is disrespectful of solid facts is often only too apt to make a fool of himself if, in interpreting the TAT (Structured Interview responses) he gives free rein to his imagination. The future of the TAT (Structured Interview responses) hangs on the possibility of perfecting the interpreter (psychology's forgotten instrument) more than it does on perfecting the material."

E. *Rationale*

1. THEORETICAL CONSIDERATIONS

The Structured Interview is at once a Projective Test and a Psychiatric Interview. It is a Projective Test in that it facilitates the disclosing of unconscious feelings and ideas, through projecting them, in Part I, onto a "make-believe person" (the own-sex drawing previously made in the Draw-a-Person Test.) It is a psychiatric interview in that, in Part II, the same questions (many of them intimate and personal) are asked with respect to the subject himself.

When the Structured Interview is used in conjunction with the Rorschach, it may be that it contributes a difference in stress or focus. The focus in the Rorschach is primarily on depth analysis and on unconscious and preconscious levels. The focus in the Structured Interview is primarily on the conscious level (the self-concept; the ego goal; and sometimes the awareness of ego loss or diminution).

It seems possible that the Structured Interview will more readily and effectively accomplish certain of the aims of the Psychiatric Interview. These aims Saul[3] had in mind, when listing the important aspects which such an interview should cover he said (p. 81), "Since the analyst works with the major motivational forces in the patient, it is important to include these in the history,—"The patient will be fully aware of certain of these emotional forces, and of their operations. Of others, he will have but a glimmering awareness, and of still others, and of the processes connected with them, he will be unconscious."

These "major motivational forces," as listed by Saul (pp. 83-4) are given below, so that they may be readily reviewed in relation to the Structured Interview responses.

a. "Sexual history."

b. "One great force which underlies neurosis is dependence. The history should cover, as explicitly as seems indicated, the interplay between the forces toward dependence and those toward independence."

c. "The same applies to the patient's need for love and to his receptivity and demands, as opposed to his capacity for giving energy, love, interest, and sympathetic understanding to others."

d. "Also vital are feelings of inferiority and their sources, and egotism, narcissism, and competitiveness toward parents and siblings and their representatives."

e. "The superego should be explored: the kind of training and how the patient adapted himself to it; the state of shame and guilt, and the kinds of imagoes the patient has. This is of immeasurable importance for the prediction of the course of the transference and the success of treatment."

f. "The history of hostility is as indispensable as the various aspects of the libidinal history. Asking the patient about his temper, his anger, his resentments from earliest childhood to the present time, usually brings out highly significant information."

g. "Mechanisms of flight, including regressive trends, should be explored."

h. "For neurotic symptoms to be present, the nuclear emotional pattern must have been warped to some extent by injurious influences during childhood. We seek the nature of those traumatic influences and their effect upon the core of the patient's personality."

i. "Throughout the taking of the history the interviewer does well to notice explicitly the ego functions, the relation of the ego to the forces of id and superego, its sensitivity, its most prominent defense mechanism, its grasp of reality, its aesthetic and intellectual capacities, and its judgment, will, and strength."

2. CONTRIBUTIONS OF THE STRUCTURED INTERVIEW TO THE PROJECTIVE TEST BATTERY

The question, "Why still another test?" is relevant at this point. This is not the first "test" which has attempted to elicit personal information with the aid of drawings and ensuing questions. The Draw-a-Person Test already referred to and the House-Tree-Person Test[4] include such a list of questions. True, in these cases, the questions asked are primarily about the drawing which has been made, only certain specific questions being asked about the subject himself.* Clearly, if the Structured Interview merely offered another way of doing substantially the same thing which these and other projective tests so skillfully do, it would have no justification for being. It is felt, however, that it *does* contribute

---

* Machover (supra) says on pages 30 and 32, "A brief series of questions relating to the subject's social and sexual attitudes are included.—He is further asked to identify which of the statements he made may refer to himself as well as the figure. When used for diagnostic or therapeutic purposes the associations may be extended and adapted to problems specific to the individual."

several additional things; the most readily observable being the amazing ease and fluency with which the subject talks about himself. Seemingly, there is stirred up a need to do so which is experienced sufficiently strongly to enable him to overcome his reluctance to so doing.

What is there about this interview technique which may facilitate this readiness? While no definitive answer is possible, the following points may offer at least partial answers:

a. The spirit in which this interviewing is done (the feelings and attitudes of the person doing the interviewing). Today, counter-transference reactions are felt to be as important aspects to evaluate in interview techniques as they are in the more formally labeled "therapy sessions."**[5] In the technique under consideration here, no less than in psychotherapy itself, negative reactions (whether conscious or unconscious) may prejudice results anywhere from diminishing returns to a point of no return. As White-house[6] puts it: "The personal interaction between examiner and examinee constitutes the most vital part of this (psychiatric) examination." Unless the interviewer is truly concerned with the patient, not only as a human being with *problems*, but as a *human being;* unless he is capable (because of his empathetic reactions) of creating a general atmosphere of sympathy and understanding, he wastes his time and the patient's time in giving the Structured Interview.

b. In a deeper sense, the subject's readiness to respond may also be a function of Patient-Examiner relationship. Lending oneself seriously to the test requirement that one "pretend" that a drawing one has made is a person one knows well enough to talk intimately about, requires a certain willingness to "play" unashamedly in front of another person; safe from any possibility of mockery. Any one who has ever been honored, through being accepted by some child as "safe" in this way, knows of the faith in him which is implicit before the child can, without self-consciousness, dramatize his phantasies before him. In the case of the adult, even more truly than in that of the child, the giving of

---

** See Gill, Neuman and Redlich, "The Dynamic Intake Interview is based on . . . a comprehension of, and use of transference and counter-transference."

this faith must depend both on the capacity for basic trust, as Erikson[7] has defined that term, and on a recognition that the examiner *is* one to be thus trusted.

This also implies that, to an even greater extent than the other tests call for it, the "good examiner" in this case must be a "giving person." It may well be that, if one has not matured to a point where true giving is possible, he will somehow feel "threatened" as he asks these questions.

c. It seems possible that the position of this test in the test battery may also facilitate this readines to talk. It is felt that the Structured Interview is best given immediately after the Rorschach, for the following two reasons:

First; when, as is frequently done, the responses of the Rorschach are recorded on the left side of a vertically folded paper, followed, by completing the inquiry on the right side of the same paper, it would seem as though the subject must recognize that again there will be a "second part" in the Structured Interview, when the responses to the "person" are recorded on the left side of a similarly folded paper. Being "set" for the second part may actually arouse the expectation (and the hope) that, in the second part, he may somehow be encouraged to talk about himself.

Second; the stirring up of unconscious impulses and wishes referred to by Schafer[8] as facilitating psychoanalytic interpretation of Rorschach responses would also seem to provide a good mental set for the overcoming of certain of the restraints and inhibitions relative to talking intimately about one's self to a stranger. For it seems very possible that the patient, who, in common with most human beings, has suffered from a sense of loneliness; from an awareness of a world that does not care, may, on some level, be feeling "All my life I have wanted to sit down and talk to someone who really cares how I feel about these things, and when finally someone *does* sit down and ask me these questions, whom do we talk about? A make-believe person!" With this comes the all but verbalized question, "But what about me?"

d. It may be that the comparisons with childhood situations which occur in so many of the questions, as Part I is administered, create a setting in which the subject can look back, with a new-found insight into childhood problem areas. This, then, may become strengthened in Part II, through a sudden linking of his past with his current problems and difficulties.

e. Another reason why the Structured Interview readily elicits personalized information may be due to the way many people (particularly during adolescence) have managed to satisfy the need to talk about themselves, under the disguised heading of "someone I know." Many efforts to get help or advice start with the words, "A friend of mine had the following thing happen to him." The Structured Interview merely formalizes this indirect way of asking for help.

Sometimes it actually happens that a wish to talk about himself, which has been largely hidden from awareness (possibly because of fear of disappointment of the wish) breaks through to a point where it is borne in on the subject, to his own surprise, that he has, in fact, *been* speaking about himself. This sudden awareness may actually then result in new realizations, possibly even a more conscious acceptance of the need for therapy, as the recognition that he really *has* a problem dawns on him.

f. The implications inherent in the fact that this is a "test" situation may constitute another reason for the readiness to respond:

(1) The examination experience of school days has, we may assume, produced some need to "do well" in a test ("do well" in this case meaning to lend one's self to the test situation; cooperating to the best of one's ability).

(2) The essential impersonalness of the test situation. True, seemingly personal questions are asked, but the "student," in recognizing this as a test, also recognizes that the test objective is not to pry (in any personal sense) into his background, feeling or ideas. This is done for examination purposes only; a qualification which, somehow, makes the most personal questions impersonal.

F. *Test Validation*

At this point, a word should be said regarding the question of test validation. To date, no experimental studies have been done with this technique. It is in its infancy and is offered here somewhat in the spirit in which an infant is shown to visitors. Nothing is known as yet about its future, but even in its infancy it speaks, as it were, for itself. As to the rest, time will tell. Naturally, it is hoped that validating work will, in the future, be undertaken with this technique. However, even at this stage it is felt that in some measure "it speaks for itself" in the sense that all psychiatric interviews speak for themselves.

Possibly, however, even were considerable work to be done in validation studies, certain uncertainties would remain uncertain; as stubbornly resistant to statistical procedures as are many psychoanalytic problems. It may well be that no frontal attack is possible in these areas; we may have to be willing to make inferences and to set up hypotheses on the basis of our understanding of unconscious processes, and of the recurrently experienced need to defend one's self against anxiety.

Again a quotation from Murray (page 14) seems appropriate: "To guide the intuitions of the interpreter . . . . all that can be offered . . . . are a few guiding principles coming out of several years of practical experience. The testing of these and other suggestions constitutes a program for the future. In any event, the conclusions that are reached by an analysis of these stories must be regarded as good leads or working hypotheses to be verified by other methods, rather than as proved facts."

G. *Reliability*

Murray, considering the question of reliability, continues (page 18), "Seeing that the TAT responses reflect the fleeting mood, as well as the present life situation of the subject, we should not expect the repeat reliability of the test to be high, even though the bulk of the content objectifies tendencies and traits that are relatively constant. Data on this point are lacking." The same may be said with reference to the Structured Interview.

H. *Suggested Research*

The following suggestions for research occur at this time. Since no systematic research has, to date, been carried out, other fruitful possibilities may suggest themselves to various workers:

a. *A study of structured interview reactions of various nosologic groups.*

The writer, in her own thinking, sees this less as a differential diagnostic study than as an effort to learn more about the different experiences (objective and subjective) which, it may be, played a part in the development in one or another direction.

b. *An exploration into possible meanings in differences in the capacity, or the willingness, to lend oneself to the requirements of this technique.*

It has already been stated that there is a difference in the extent to which various individuals are able (or willing) to "play the game" required in Part I. There is also a difference in the extent to which others restrict themselves to answering only with reference to their own feelings and experiences. Some immediately announce that they will talk about themselves, refusing to be swayed from this position. Others suddenly realize that they have done this, after a considerable number of the questions have been asked. Still others only mention their awareness, after they have been informed that they are now to be asked the same questions about themselves. They may mention this either with sudden insight, or with the implication that they assumed that this had been taken for granted. Occasionally, subjects never indicate such an awareness.

Is there a difference between individuals who react in these various ways? If so, what can we make of this difference? One example of such a difference seems worth citing. The writer has several times noted that subjects with marked narcissistic character defects have refused to lend themselves to the "game" part of this test. They have indicated their willingness to answer the question with reference to themselves. But in spite of adequate imagination, they clearly cannot or will not think in terms of *the other person*. For them, there is only *the self*.

c. *An investigation of differences resulting from split-half control of the procedure of administration.*

It might be interesting to study two groups, one to be given the Structured Interview in the way described in these pages; the second to be asked the various questions about the *Self* first (in the psychiatric interview manner). This would be followed by the questions about the *Person*, with the request that the subject now "make believe" that the drawing is a real person. It may be that the questions on which he blocked or became evasive when asked about himself are answered freely or quite differently in the case of the *Person*, and that additional insights may develop out of this.

d. *An investigation of differences between responses to own-sex and other-sex drawings.*

Since, in many instances, we suspect that the other-sex drawing may in varying degrees also be an identification figure, a study might be rewarding in which the questions are not only asked about the own-sex picture, but that of the opposite sex as well; to be followed by what then would become Part III (the questions about the self).

e. *An investigation of possible discrepancies between Rorschach, and/or TAT findings and those offered by the Structured Interview.*

To date, no significant discrepancies have been noted. However, this has not been systematically studied.

f. *An investigation of possible positive relationship between "giving" in the Structured Interview and favorable prognosis in therapy.*

It seems possible that, in the course of the Structured Interview administration, certain favorable predictive reactions can be recognized. Among these might be capacity to develop insight into one's own dynamics; capacity to form a therapeutic relationship; capacity to develop a recognition of a need for help.

g. *Experimentation with an abbreviated form.*

Since the Structured Interview, as here given, takes approximately an hour to administer it may well be that, if it is to be included in a test battery, the administration time will have to be reduced. This seems worth attempting, since rigidity in administration does not appear to serve any useful end. It has already been suggested that flexibility in the use of language seems desirable. In the same way, certain questions may, on some occasions, be productive; on others, less productive. Thus, the questions about childhood need not be routinely asked, but only in those situations where it is felt that a possible difference between *then* and *now* might add some significant insight. Other questions may also be omitted, or modified, depending on the need as the examiner sees it.

h. *Possible time saver, in cases where the examiner becomes the therapist.*

It seems possible that, in the course of the Structured Interview experience, the therapist is established as a "giving person" in the eyes of the patient. The memory of that early "giving" may linger on, reducing the resistance which at first the silence of the therapist sometimes evokes.

I. *Suggestions for Evaluating Structured Interview Responses*

What facts can we learn from these Structured Interview responses and, considerably more important, what inferences can we draw? It should be emphasized at the outset of this section that the actual *facts* discovered are relatively few and, in general, not of a nature which would require a special kind of interview technique to elicit. Such questions as age, marital status, conditions of health, education, siblings, etc., are an inevitable part of all interviewing.

However, we also learn a second kind of fact, namely, how a subject experiences many of the situations. Such a question as "Was there a favorite child in your family?" is not necessarily factually answered, but it *does* give an answer to the subject's feeling about these things.

Mainly, however, what concerns us is a third, more subtle kind of information which this technique often elicits. Sullivan[9] speaks of the psychiatric interview as "designed to discover obscure difficulties in living, difficulties which the patient does not understand clearly, and about which he misleads himself and others." He adds, "The difficulties stand out more clearly and meaningfully when one grasps the sort of person the patient is, what he does, and why he does it."

What are the "obscure difficulties" to which the Structured Interview responses point? What inferences can be drawn? What hypotheses advanced? On what can we base these inferences and hypotheses? In the attempt to answer these questions, three different methods of test evaluation are dealt with. It is through the interrelation of these types of evaluation that interpretation develops.

1. INTER-TEST EVALUATION

a. Inter-test Similarity:

Let us first consider the situation in which the "person" of Part I and the "self" of Part II are the same. It may be added parenthetically that the subject does not always state this identity in words, or indeed be fully aware that this is so. He may merely make an occasional slip, such as saying "I" when he meant to say "he." More often, however, he suddenly arrives at the startled recognition that this has taken place. Sometimes he verbalizes this with considerable surprise. Identification is, of course, actually expected in this projective material. Murray, in speaking of the rationale of the TAT (p. 1) says, "The fact that stories collected in this way often reveal significant components of personality is dependent on the . . . . tendency of those who write stories to draw on the fund of their experiences, and express their sentiments and needs, whether conscious or unconscious." The interpretation of drawings, when used as projective tests, makes the assumption that the "person" *is* the "self." But it is important to wonder which aspect of the self is being portrayed; the ego-ideal; the hated self; the feared self; the self he would like to be but dare not? In each individual case, the picture presented should give the clue to the answer. It makes a difference whether the "person" and the "self" are alike in being upstanding or self-abnegating; achieving or failing; ego-syntonic or ego-alien.

b. Inter-test Differences:

Occasionally the two individuals are entirely and convincingly different. No over-all explanation of the meaning of this seems possible. The dichotomous descriptions themselves may, however, serve as clues. Is "the person" what the patient himself wished to be, but was not? Is it what he feared to be, but could not entirely avoid being? Is it what he secretly wanted to be but dared not work for? Or, if none of these things, what else might these two diametrically opposite people stand for?

c. Partly Similar — Partly Different:

Sometimes the differences are only true in part; in certain of the situations described the individuals are strikingly alike. Again, it can only be said that an attempt should be made to evaluate the areas of likeness and of difference in terms of what has been suggested above.

2. INTRA-TEST COMPARISONS

Second, there are the inferences to be drawn by intra-test discrepancies or contradictions. Certain test items (listed below) would, one might expect, elicit the same type of response. When the opposite occurs, we may raise a kind of mental eyebrow, alerting ourselves to the possibility that there is more to the picture than the reply suggests (even when both responses are sincerely given). A list of the questions in which agreement would seem expected is given below:

(1) Questions 2 and 3 (Ideally there should be some relationship between educational level and type of occupation).

(2) Questions 3 and 4 (One would expect a good student to go further in his schooling than a mediocre or poor one).

(3) Questions 5a and 5b (One would expect a child's behavior at home and in school to be fairly consistent).

(4) Questions 8, 9 and 10 (Health, appetite and sleep should, we would assume, be positively related).

(5) Questions 11, 2, and 3 (The more intelligent individual should, ideally, do better in school and have a higher status type of occupation).

(6) Questions 13 and 16 (While one would not expect a one-to-one correspondence between calmness and happiness, generally speaking, a positive relationship would be anticipated).

(7) Questions 15 and 17 (It would seem that in general, a popular person is one who likes to spend his time with people, and that the opposite is true about an unpopular person).

(8) Questions 7, 21, and 28 (Without being able precisely to pinpoint it, one would expect some positive relationship between attitudes towards bringing up one's child, and one's own childhood ways of experiencing parental attitudes).

(9) Questions 13, 23, and 24 (Some relationship would be expected to exist between general calmness, irritability and proneness to anger).

(10) Questions 16 and 24 (One might also anticipate some relationship between a happy or unhappy nature and the individual's judgment as to the kinds of situations which produce a pleasant or a good mood).

3. Ego Identity Struggle

The third way of evaluating the Structured Interview is more complex and requires some preliminary statements. Essentially it derives from Erikson's[10] work on ego developments, and from his stress on the ego identity struggle; a struggle which he sees as an intrinsic part of psycho-social development. As Erikson defines it, each developmental phase, adjustedly achieved, concurrently becomes a period of ego growth and development; one in which the ego adds to its previous identifications certain newly libidinized images which derive from the expanded world unfolding before him. When this interacting growth is arrested, a blocking in ego development occurs simultaneously with the psycho-social fixation. In times of stress, regression to the developmental period prior to the trauma goes hand in hand with regression to a more infantile ego state. Erikson considers eight developmental phases; the first, infancy; the last, mature age. Between are the various periods of childhood, adolescence and adulthood through which the individual passes, and during which the psychic resources necessary for taking the next step are acquired.*

---

* This is not the first time that the writer has had reason to acknowledge indebtedness to Erikson for his work on ego identity. In a paper called "The Use of the Rorschach in Preventive Mental Hygiene"[11] she sought to develop a way in which the Rorschach insights might be used to enable the child successfully to climb the various steps Erikson so beautifully describes in his "Childhood and Society." (op. cit.)

As we read the Structured Interview responses, it is hypothesized that we are witnessing the various successes and part-successes, as well as the traumas and frustrations which, in their interplay, determine the strength, the fixation or regression points, and the final ego level in each individual case. This will be explained more fully in the sample case which follows.

II. Illustrative Case Study

A. *Structured Interview Responses*

MAKE-BELIEVE PERSON	SELF
1. (Age?) "18."	1. "25."
2. (Occupation?) "Professional ball player."	2. "Student."
3. (Education?) "He finished high school."	3. "I had 2½ years of college."
4. a. (Type of student?) "Average."	4. a. "I was below average in high school and average in college."
b. (Classroom behavior?) Long hesitation—kept saying, "Gee—I don't know." Finally said, "Let's have him quiet."	b. "I was very quiet—but wasn't bad within the group. I had a good group of boys—sports particularly."
5. (Home behavior?) "He was pretty friendly at home—quite talkative at home."	5. "I don't know—I had five brothers—I mean five brothers and sisters. I never thought of it much. I talked quite a lot. Kept things to myself though."
6. (Parent Identification?)	6.
a. (Like which parent?) "Well, he is pretty much like both."	a. "My father died when I was 3½, so I don't know."
b. (How?) "He is like his father in that he likes sports, but he is like his mother also in that he has her original ideas—and follows them through."	b.
c. (Preferred parent?) "Well, he seems to get along with his mother best."	c. "Pretty good relationship with mother but wasn't close to her actually."
d. (Preferred parent in childhood?) "His mother."	d.

e. (Religious Upbringing?)
Strict.

e. "Quite strict—on the outside more than the inside."
Q. (How do you mean?) "Well—I shouldn't say that." (sighs) Asks, "Do you know what I mean? It wasn't well integrated into my personality."

7. (Health?)

7.

a. (Now?) "He's very healthy—pretty healthy."

a. Asks, "My physical health?" (Reassured—"any way you want to answer it.") "Well—I'm here—so—" Q. (Physical health?) "not bad—don't have the desire for it to be much better." Q. "Didn't that explain itself?"

b. (In childhood?) "We'll say he had a handicap."

b. "I was very, very thin and tall."

c. (Parents fussy?) "Yes, sort of."

c. "Very concerned."

d. (How?) "Well, she worried in a general way."

d. "She was concerned with all of us —all the kids, just concerned about us—very, very concerned—and yet, she wasn't close—it's hard to explain."

8. (Appetite?)

8.

a. (Now?) Good appetite

a. "Just fair now."

b. (In childhood?) Good appetite.

b. "Very, very, good, exceptional."

9. (Sleep?)

9.

a. (Now?) "No difficulty, falls asleep as he hits the bed."

a. "Just fair."

b. (In childhood?) "It might have been a little harder when he was a child."

b. "Guess I fell asleep OK."

10. (Intelligence?)

10.

a. (How intelligent?)
"Average."

a. "I'd say average."

b. (Best functioning period?)
"No best period." (Q)
"Yes, equally good all the time."

b. "I think when I was real small—maybe up to the 7th grade."

c. (In what way?)

c. "Because I was always put on competition and we used to get medals for doing good, both in school work and in athletic competition, and that always spurred me on. And after that (7th grade), that started the masturbation period." (Explains that his mother used to scold him for masturbating and that he did it in secret.)

11. (Disposition?)—Long pause—"Well, say he's less calm than average."

11. "Terrible—not calm! The furthest from calmness. It's holding me back."

12. (How likes to spend time?) "Spends time doing things he likes to do."

12. "Well, I like to be with people—with a family—I like to be around kids and have dates. I like being with a family best—someone close to me—a relative or someone. I'm calmest then."

13. (Popularity? Do people like him?) "He's not too popular. He's a non-conformist—as far as kids can be."

13. "They *say* they do." (Long pause) "I don't draw people to me at all. I don't have the personality that draws people to me especially—I'm not a popular figure, even in a small group."

14. (Nature?)

   a. (Happy?) "He's very happy."
   b. (Happiest period?) "Well, I said he had a handicap—I said he was a non-conformist—so the happiest was when he was surest that he accepted his handicap and his own particular nature—t h a t which made him a non-conformist. When he was sure of himself—didn't care what people thought—he was happiest."
   c. (In which way?)
   d. (Hardest period?)

14.

   a. "I'm unhappy."
   b. "Gee, I don't know." (long pause) "I don't know . . . . Guess when I was a kid."

   c. "I don't know."
   d. "The thing that comes to my mind was when my older brother, Tom, slapped me. It's strange because it didn't hurt so much really —and Tom isn't a bit that kind of a person. He's a wonderful brother —my favorite of all my brothers. It happened when I was about eight or nine. He had a girl

friend—and I liked her very much, but one day I said something about her. I don't remember what it was—but it must have been fresh, and Tom hit me right across the face. Somehow—I can't forget it. Once in a while I think of it— and then I think something strange—something I don't understand. I think, 'I wish you had hit me much harder, Tom, much, much harder.'"

15. (Sociable?) "Well, by his nature he likes to do things alone—or with one or two persons, but he likes people. It isn't that he doesn't like people— he likes people very much."

15. "It depends on the mood—by nature I'm kind of alone-er. Then there's the other extreme—a mood I often get in, then we run up against the problem I have told you of . . . I don't believe a word I said. I'm thinking of the year I worked in a factory. I was very sociable. I believe it's the opposite. I believe I am very sociable —talkative. I think I'm inhibited and that's what makes it seem as though I'm the other way."

16. (Best thing?) "Well, for one, he sticks to his convictions, religious or otherwise. He may falter once in a while, but in general he sticks to his convictions despite other people—or other things."

16. "Gee, I don't know what it is." (Long pause) "Best thing is I'm trying to know myself and my nature."

17. (Worst thing?) "Well, maybe his disposition—and it may be because of his nature—it might be lack of charity."

17. "Egotistical, selfish, full of pride, I guess. It's holding me back,—pride— selfish that is—you know."

18. a. (Married?) "No, he's only eighteen. He would be single."

   b. (Is marriage anticipated?) "Yes."

18. a. "No."

   b. "Yes."

19. a. (Children?)

   b. (Anticipate children?) "Yes, he hopes to have lots of children."

19. a.

   b. "Yes."

20. (Upbringing of children?)

    a.

    b. (Anticipate bringing them up in the way he was brought up or differently?) "Well, this guy is a happy guy we said, so he will probably bring them up the way he was brought up."

21. (Wish?) Asks, "Any wish?" (Long pause) "Hmm! I would say that he could be more sociable—could help people more—be more sociable in that sense."

22. (Nerves?) "Well, he's quite impatient because of his nature—and—I don't know what gets on his nerves —unreasonable people—stupidity."

23. (What puts him in a good mood?)

    a. (Now?) "Good music—walking alone at night—maybe—or with another person—or just talking with another person about the higher things in life."

    b. (In childhood?) "Sports, music, being with his parents."

24. (Fears?)

    a. (Now?) Long pause—puts head in hands to think. "He's not afraid of very much. There's very little he's afraid of."

    b. (In childhood?) "Oh, that was different. He was afraid because he had his—he was afraid of people, maybe. He was afraid to mix because of his handicap; that probably provoked the things I have said about him before."

25. (What kind of things make him angry?)

    a. (Now?) "The same things—unreasonableness and the biased opinions of others."

20.

    a.

    b. "I didn't have a father—so that would eliminate that question."

21. "To be happy."

22. "Snobs—people that—oh, the same thing I said before. I'm not saying I don't provoke it, not voluntarily— but—"

23.

    a. "A story, any friendly situation— I don't know exactly—a happy situation."

    b.

24.

    a. Long pause—"It's on the tip of my fingers, but I can't explain it. —I'm afraid of myself—certainly not afraid of truth."

    b.

25.

    a. "Oh, injustice."

b. (In childhood? "Well, when people made fun of him because he had a handicap—and—not injustice;—I don't think that's what I mean—but the littleness of people—not that they laughed, but they would annoy him by looking the other way on the street—little social snobberies, and not only because he had his handicap, but because he was a non-conformist."

b. "I guess the same thing. People who didn't seem to think I was as good as they were."

26. (Ambition?)

   a. (Asks, Now?) "To have a wife and a family."

   b. (In childhood?) "Well, until he found himself there—at that one moment—he probably wanted to have a lot of foolish things, maybe revenge on those people, or to be a great ball player. But he wanted those things to show what he could do, but now he no longer wants that."

26.

   a. "Right now, to do a good job in my work and to enjoy it. But then also to get married and have a family."

   b. "To be good in sports and to do well in the competitions—be a good ball player."

27. (Chief problem?)

   a. "Well, he's a man now, so we'll say that even though he has his firm convictions, every once in a while he weakens and there's a tendency for him to do things—not for the object implied, but for a show piece or for some egotistical satisfaction."

   b.

   c. (In childhood?) "To understand his handicap—its complications and to overcome it and to get along with people."

27.

   b.

   c.

28. a. (Siblings?) "I kind of picture this guy as the only one in a family. I don't know why. I think he should have brothers or sisters."

   b. (Relationship to siblings?)

28. a. "Yes, six children."

   b. "Close to all."

c. (In childhood?)

c. "We were living out of town—we were a pretty close unit in a way —family problems but not individual problems. We didn't talk about those. I don't know why— the opportunity was there. I guess we were all like that. Don't know why."

29. a. (Favorite child?)

29. a. "No, actually I don't believe so."

b. (Which?)

b.

c. (Of one or both parents?)

c.

d. (How did he feel about it?)

d.

30. a. (Grandparents living?) "We'll say no."

30. a. "No, both dead."

b. (Grandparents living when he was a child?) "Let's say they died when he was young."

b. "Yes."

c. (Relationship to them?)

c. "I don't remember, but I guess my grandmother was close to me. She tried to be awfully friendly—I remember that she was too busy to be any closer." (Q). "No, she didn't live with us."

31. (What *one* thing would he like to change in his life?) "To have accepted his handicap and his nonconformist nature wholly, sooner than he did."

31. "That's a bad question! Well, I wish I had a father, but you mean if I didn't have, and had to wish? I guess if I had accepted things as they were I would have gotten along better."

32. (Any additions?) "No, nothing else special."

32. "Well, I'm having a great deal of trouble with my work, can't concentrate hardly at all. And I have trouble about girls—I feel so uncomfortable when I'm with them. I never can think what to say or do. I always imagine they think I'm a drip."

B. *Structured Interview Interpretive Evaluation*

In order to arrive at an interpretive evaluation of this Structured Interview protocol, each of the areas of evaluation described earlier must be dealt with in turn. They are listed below, in order to facilitate the task of keeping them in mind.

1. Inter-test Comparison
   a. Similarity
   b. Differences
   c. Same-Different
2. Intra-test Comparison
   a. Person
   b. Self
3. Ego Identity Struggle

1. INTER-TEST COMPARISON

a. *Similarity*

There are six particulars in which the "person" and the "self" are thought of as being the same—1) both were quiet in school; 2) both are of average intelligence; 3) both are unmarried but hope to marry in the future; 4) both are looking forward to having children; 5) as children both were "angry when people were "snobbish" to them; 6) both sets of grandparents are described as no longer living.

INTERPRETIVE IMPRESSION

The suggestion is that, during the growing-up years (in spite of a certain shyness and docility of behavior), there was a capacity for anger under rejection. At present there is relatively low self-esteem (only average intelligence is conceded). Moreover, the expressed wish to be married is still not actualized.

b. *Differences:*

There are 23 items in which the "person" and "self" are different.

(1) The "person" is a late adolescent; the "self" a young adult.

(2) The "person" is a professional ball player; the "self" a student.

(3) The educational level is higher for the "self" (2½ years of college as contrasted with being a high school graduate).

(4) The high school grades, however, were lower in the case of the "self" (below average versus average).

(5) The "person" resembles both parents; in the case of the "self" the answer is, "My father died when I was 3½."

(6) The "person" had a handicap (never defined or made more specific); the "self" is described without handicap, but as "very, very thin" as a child.

(7 & 8) The "person" has a good appetite and slept well; in the case of the "self" both are "just fair."

(9) However, the "person" in childhood had a harder time falling asleep than did the "self."

(10) The "person" has functioned equally well throughout life; the "self" functioned at his best when he was "real small, maybe up to the 7th grade."

(11) The "person" likes to spend his time doing things *he* likes to do; the "self" likes to "be with people, someone close, a relative."

(12) The "person" is very happy; the "self" unhappy.

(13) The "person" was happiest when he didn't care what others thought; the "self" when he was "a kid."

(14) The worst experience in the life of the "person" was when people started snubbing him; for the "self" it was when his big brother hit him for making some "fresh" remarks about his girl friend.

(15) The best thing about the "person" is that he "sticks" to his convictions; in the case of the "self" it consists of trying to know "myself and my nature."

(16) The worst thing about the "person" is lack of charity; in the "self" it is being "egotistical—full of pride."

(17) The "person" intends to bring his prospective children up as he was brought up; the "self" (unable to answer the question directly) merely replies, "I don't have a father—so that would eliminate that question."

(18) The "person's" wish is to help people; the "self's" wish is to be happy.

(19) Stupid and unreasonable people get on the "person's" nerves; snobs are the irritants for the "self."

(20) The "person" is almost unafraid; the "self" replies, "I'm afraid of myself."

(21) A good mood is created for the "person" by "music, walking alone at night or with another person, or just talking to another person about the higher things of life." It is a "story—a friendly situation: a happy situation" which puts the "self" in a good mood.

(22) The "person" considers his greatest problem an occasional tendency to do things for a show, for some egotistical reason. The "self" speaks in terms of a yearning to soothe or overcome his tense and unhappy feelings.

(23) The "person" is an only child; the "self"—one of six siblings.

INTERPRETIVE IMPRESSION

The over-all impression, as one studies the differences between the "self" and the "person," is clearly in favor of the "person." He is more robust; he has more self-confidence; he is happy; outgoing, unafraid; a good student, and in general, a well functioning and satisfied individual. What, then, shall we make of the suggestion of certain marked problems, occurring in the "person's" developmental years? Why did being snubbed affect him so much that it became his "worst experience"? Why, as a child did he have a harder time falling asleep than did the "self"? What does his being an only child (as contrasted with the "Self's" large family of siblings) mean? What is the handicap which with so little visible effect, seemingly beclouded the "person's" childhood? And why on the other hand, did the "self" after an initial good period, start showing disturbance and interference after 7th grade?

It seems possible that the first four questions asked above actually suggest some strange discrepancy or contradiction which has here intruded itself into the generalized picture of a well-functioning personality. It is as though, without the patient having intended it, the sense of a "handicap" is so tied up with his self-concept that it intrudes even into his phantasy of the "wished for" self; (his image of the "person" he might have been had he not had the "handicap"). Might this "handicap," we must ask ourselves, have been the death of the father? Might it have seemed through the growing up years as though inevitably he *must* be snubbed, because not to have a father is to be "different"; and in some way set apart? Since, however, the picture is of being an object of scorn and not of pity, we further hazard the guess that on some level the idea of not having a father was linked to something that justifies scorn (some "badness" in himself, associated with this "handicap.") If the child he then was experienced guilt in this connection, the difficulty in falling asleep would be accounted for.

But why did these things change? Why did the "wished for self" (the "person") throw off this guilt? And why did the "self" start having difficulties and interferences, approximately from the 7th grade on?

We can only hypothesize, we cannot know. However, if at this age something occurred to re-activate a repressed childhood guilt, then the sense of inferiority and unworthiness from which he has long suffered would break through to consciousness, and therefore no longer need to be inappropriately associated with the "wished for self." The "person" therefore would be set free, to become happy and well functioning. The "self" would shoulder the burden of guilt.

As to the "only child"; might this be another unconscious wish? An only child does not have to share love and attention. If an individual feels himself already deprived ("he has no father") might he not, even more than most children, phantasy a situation where he is at least the recipient of his mother's undivided attention?

c. *Same-Different:*

Eleven questions are responded to with partial similarity, but in part, they are also different.

(1) The "person" and the "self" are both "quite talkative," *but* the "self" kept things to himself.

(2) They both had a strict religious upbringing; *but* in the case of the "self," it was not well integrated into his personality.

(3) They were both healthy, *but* in the case of the "self" a distinction is made between the physical health and whatever the (unhealthy) thing is that "brings him here."

(4) In both cases childhood health was a cause of concern, *but* in the case of the "self," the mother was "*very, very* concerned."

(5) Both had good appetites as children, *but* in the case of the "self," it was "*very, very* good—exceptional."

(6) Both are less calm than average, *but* in the case of the "self," the lack of calmness is "terrible—the furthest from calmness."

(7) Both are unpopular, the "person" because he is a nonconformist, the "self" because he doesn't have "the personality that draws people."

(8) Both are initially described as preferring to do things alone, *but* in the case of the "self" this is then completely denied and the opposite is affirmed.

(9) Both hope to marry and have children, *but* in the case of the "self," the need to achieve is given priority.

(10) Both were close to the grandmother in childhood, but in the case of the "self" there is the added realization that she "tried to be awfully friendly, but she was too busy."

(11) Both would like to be able to have accepted the "handicap" *but* in the case of the "self," the thing he would particularly like to change is the loss of the father.

Repeatedly, the "self" is more troubled; unfortunate things are so in greater degree. The intensity of the deprivation, the loneliness, the disabling conflicts, and the "handicap" are stronger and more pervasive.

INTERPRETIVE IMPRESSION

The striking thing about the kind of differences depicted here is the frequency with which they are a matter of intensity, not contradiction: 1) the "person's" mother was concerned about her children, but *very, very* concerned in the case of "the self"; 2) both had good appetites but in the case of the "self," it was "very, very good;" 3) both are less calm than average, but in the case of the "self" it's "terrible, the furthest thing from calm;" 4) both would like to have accepted their "handicap" more successfully, but in the case of the "self" there is still the open, almost aching, sense of loss.

The second striking aspect in these differences, is the qualitatives differences suggested in some of the answers: 1) both were talkative, but, the "self" in spite of this, was secretive; 2) both had a religious upbringing, but it was never integrated into the "self's" personality; 3) both were physically healthy, but the "self" feels himself beset by emotional problems; 4) both are described as unpopular, but in the case of the "self," it is because of an unlikeable personality; 5) both were described as close to the grandmother, but in the case of the "self" there is recognition that this was not so in actuality ("she was too busy").

There is a third aspect to these differences; some evidence of current conflict (outspokenly, in the self-statement relating to "what brought me here"; implicitly, in a need to defer the wish to marry, common to both, until he can do a good job in his work and enjoy it.)

The over-all impression is of acute and painful awareness of problem areas, including feelings of inferiority and conflict.

2. Intra-test Comparison

a. *Person:*

In five sets of answers, some contradiction or discrepancy is suggested:

(1) The "person" is quiet in school *but* quite talkative at home.

(2) He had a handicap as a child, *yet* functioned equally well in all periods of his life.

(3) He is less calm than average, *but* very happy.

(4) He is very happy, *but* has a handicap and is a non-conformist, so that he is happiest "when he doesn't care what people think of him."

(5) He best enjoys doing things alone, *but* he wishes he could be more sociable.

INTERPRETIVE IMPRESSION

Denial, as a defense mechanism, seems suggested in the following answers: (1) A handicap which does not interfere with functioning; (2) not calm, but happy, and (3) enjoys doing things alone but wishes he could be more sociable.

In addition, there is a suggestion of a sense of rejection, and defenses against it in responses (1) and (4): talkative at home *but* quiet in school; happiest when he doesn't care what people think of him.

b. *Self:*

Four times discrepancies in behavior are hinted at:

(1) "I talked quite a bit—kept things to myself though."

(2) "Pretty good relationship with mother, but not close to her actually."

(3) Sibling relationship in childhood—"Pretty close, family problems—but not individual problems discussed."

(4) "I'm a kind of alone-er—no—I believe it's the opposite —I believe I'm very sociable."

INTERPRETIVE IMPRESSION

A conflict is suggested, centering around the wish to be "close," which, possibly during high school days, became so acute as to interfere with functioning.

3. EGO IDENTITY STRUGGLE

Erikson[10] discusses this struggle in connection with eight growth periods. These will be briefly described below; each description followed by a consideration of the patient's experiences with respect to this developmental period.

a. *Basic Trust versus Mistrust:*

In discussing the dichotomy implicit in this heading Erikson says, "The assumption is that a successful struggle on the earliest social frontier of infancy, if well guided, leads to a dominant sense of—the goodness of individual existence—a sense of 'good' powers outside and inside one's self must be assumed to arise. Its negative counterpart is a diffusion of contradictory introjects and a predominance of fantasies which pretend to coerce hostile reality with omnipotent vengeance."

We are told in the Structured Interview that the "person," as a child and "until he found himself," probably "wanted to have a lot of foolish things, maybe revenge on those people who snubbed him, or to be a great musician or a *great* ball player." These needs have not entirely passed, since, "even though he's a man now and even though he has his firm convictions, every once in a while he weakens and there's a tendency for him to do things for some egotistical satisfaction."

INTERPRETIVE IMPRESSION

We may assume, then, that, even though he "became a man," some fixation point centers around this basic problem, and that at moments of tension and conflict, there is a tendency to regress.

b. *Autonomy versus Shame:*

In this stage, according to Erikson (page 99), "the obligation to achieve an identity, not only distinct but also distinctive, is apt to arouse a painful over-all ashamedness—which now adheres to one's identity as a being with a public history, exposed to age mates and leaders.

INTERPRETIVE IMPRESSION

In the Structured Interview there is a growing awareness that some difficulty with his age mates started "when I was real small, maybe in the 7th grade." He attributes this to the fact that medals were no longer given them for doing good work, adding, "They (the medals) always spurred me on." Also, "After the 7th grade—that started the masturbation period." This and the repeated references to the snubs and a sense of being ostracized, makes it clear that in this phase, again, fixation took its toll.

c. *Initiative versus Guilt:*

"When the identity crisis breaks through to the Oedipal crisis and beyond it, to a crisis of trust, the choice of a negative identity remains the only form of initiative." (*Ibid.* pp. 99 & 100.)

In the Structured Interview there is a suggestion that the brother became the father substitute and that Oedipal guilt was experienced in relation to him. "Every once in a while I think of it and then I think something strange, I think—I wish you had hit me harder, Tom—much, much harder."

INTERPRETIVE IMPRESSION

The non-conforming, hostile boy which the "person" is depicted as being, would seem the manifestation of the negative identity Erickson speaks of.

d. *Identity versus Inferiority:*

"Work paralysis is the logical sequence of a deep sense of inadequacy (regressed to a sense of basic mistrust) of one's general equipment. Such a sense of inadequacy, of course, does not usually reflect a true lack of potentials—various reasons may exclude the individual from that experimental competition in play and work through which he learns to find and to insist on *his* kind of achievement and work identity." (*Ibid.* p. 100.)

INTERPRETIVE IMPRESSION

In the Structured Interview the "self" confesses, "I'm having a great deal of trouble with my work—can't concentrate hardly at all," (verbalizing the sense of the paralyzing inadequacy which prevents the growth of self-confidence and self-esteem).

e. *Identity versus Identity Diffusion:*

"Diffusion can lead young adults toward two deceptive developments. They may foreclose their identity development by concentrating on early genital activity without intimacy, or, on the contrary, they may concentrate on social or intellectual status values which under-play the genital element." (*Ibid.* p. 101.)

INTERPRETIVE IMPRESSION

The "person" wishes "that he could be more sociable—could help people more." The "self" likes to spend his time "being with people—with a family—around kids—and have dates—I like to be with a family best, someone close to me. I'm calmest then." What puts the "person" in a good mood is "music, walking alone at night, maybe, or with another person, or just talking to another person about the higher things of life." Seemingly our young patient has concentrated on the latter of these "Identity Diffusion" alternatives.

f. *Intimacy versus Isolation:*

"That many of our patients break down at an age which is properly considered more pre-adult than post-adolescent, is explained by the fact that often only an attempt to engage in intimate fellowship and competition, or in sexual intimacy, fully reveals the latent weakness of identity.—When a youth does not resolve such strain he may isolate himself and enter, at best, only stereotyped and formalized interpersonal relations." (*Ibid.* p. 80.)

INTERPRETIVE IMPRESSION

In the Structured Interview, while the "self" "dates," our patient adds, "I don't draw people to me. I'm not a popular figure," (an expression we hypothesize, of isolation tendencies; "justified" in terms of the "rejecting" outside world). (That this "justification" does not entirely convince our patient is indicated by the statement, "He was afraid because he had his—he was afraid of people maybe. He was afraid to mix because of his handicap. That probably provoked the things I have said of him before.")

g. and h. *Intimacy, Generativity and Integrity:*

Ericson characterizes the psychosocial gains of adult (adjusted) ego development with the terms Intimacy, Generativity and Integrity, adding, "They denote a post-adolescent level of libidinal cathexes in intimate engagements; in parenthood or other forms of generativity, and finally in the most integrative experiences and values accrued from a life time." (*Ibid.* p. 110.)

Does our patient have the potentialities of achieving this adult development?

INTERPRETIVE IMPRESSION

We know that "closeness" has always been a problem. His simple statement, "I didn't have a father, so that would eliminate that question," is eloquent of a sense of irreversible loss in that area. He also speaks of his sense of lack of closeness to his mother in spite of a "pretty good relationship." Referring to his sibling relationship, he states, "We were a pretty close unit in a way— family problems but not individual problems," adding, "I don't know why, the opportunity was there. I guess we were all like that. I don't know why." Even the grandmother turned out to have "tried" rather than succeeded, "She was too busy to be any closer."

What of the prognosis? Are there suggestions that closeness can be achieved through therapy, so that eventually our patient can marry and have "lots of children" and achieve his wish to "be happy?" We think there are. Section C which follows explores the reasoning on which this belief is predicated.

C. *Integrating These Various Structured Interview Evaluations*

In undertaking this exploration, we must integrate three different sources of information: (These will be dealt with in turn.)

1. THE PATIENT'S OWN SELF-STATEMENTS CONCERNING HIS PAST
    a. He was a small child when his father died.
    b. He was the youngest of six siblings.
    c. His young childhood is recalled without awareness of emotional problems.
    d. He did well in school until the 7th grade.
    e. Around that time, in addition to a lowering of school grades, masturbation was experienced as a problem.
    f. He also started to feel snubbed and discriminated against by his school mates.
    g. He recalls, some time after this, a traumatic situation in which his older brother hit him for some "fresh" remark about the brother's girl friend.
    h. Gradually he developed feeling of inferiority, guilt and general unworthiness.
    i. He feels uncomfortable with girls.
    j. He feels himself a reluctant "alone-er."
    k. He would like to be successful vocationally.
    l. He looks forward to marriage and children.

2. Inferences Arrived at from Interpretive Impressions

    a. He managed successfully through the earlier years, because he was able to repress certain anxiety-arousing reactions.

    b. Such reactions as came to awareness, he handled either by denying their validity, or by denying that he felt anxious or disturbed. Gradually he became less and less able to carry out these mechanisms, with the result that increasingly these erstwhile repressed feelings returned to consciousness. Some sense of a "handicap," about which he became obsessively concerned, may have arisen at this period.

    c. These stirrings within himself resulted in some acting-out behavior, directed toward current significant people in his environment.

    d. This, in turn, resulted in hostile, critical reactions from these current significant people.

    e. These present-day situations received additional impact, because they re-activated the original traumatic situation.

3. Theoretical Constructs

What could this material be, which had to be repressed so early in life, and which, when acted-out with respect to a later situation, brought with it such feeling of unworthiness, inadequacy and rejection?

It has been hypothesized that the father's death was experienced by the patient as in some way due to him; to some "badness" which had made the father leave him. This initial sense of "badness," it seems possible, in some way became linked to his growing wish to have the mother all to himself (in the Structured Interview expressed by the fact that the "Person" has no siblings).

These reactions might well become so anxiety-arousing that they would perforce be repressed. This repression might later be fortified by denial mechanisms;—(far from wanting the mother all to himself, the boy he then was felt himself happy and secure only in the total family situations;—a feeling which has persisted to this day).

It may have "happened," however, that he began to feel anxious and insecure when away from the family; projecting onto strangers the critical and punitive feeling which the repression of the guilt prevented him from feeling towards himself.

4. PROGNOSIS AND TREATMENT PLANNING

What, assuming this to be so, is the outlook for this patient, so far as the future is concerned? Does therapy seem indicated, and if so, what type of therapy?

The full answer to these questions must, of course, wait the results of the Rorschach evaluation. At this point we can only speculate as follows, in terms of this material:

    a. It seems doubtful that any deep-seated changes will occur spontaneously.

    b. Therapy on an ego level, however, may enable this patient to arrive at more self-accepting and self-valuing attitudes. Moreover, since capacity for self-help is indicated, (as witness the fact that he was able to transpose the initial traumatic "bad boy, with resulting loss of father" situation, into the untraumatic "bad boy *but* no loss of big brother" situation), the possibility should be raised that increase in self-esteem may help the patient to function on a more mature level (in spite of evidence of some fixations at various earlier developmental stages.)

    c. However, since so large a part of these dynamics have remained unconscious, some doubt must be raised as to whether help on an ego level will do more than again produce a period in which functioning is adequate, and anxiety is by-passed. Should anxiety again break through, a deeper, more intensive type of analytic therapy might become necessary.

D. *Rorschach Responses*

I. 2″

1. First impression was a spider.

1. Q. (Describe) Holds card at arm's length.
"Oh, now other impressions come to mind. I can't see it as a spider. Then says, "These I think, were his arms and then the fibres of his body and the web are underneath. You can see it here. His legs· and his whole elongated body—they're all underneath."
Q. (W)

2. Then next—that it looks like some kind of fish—lobster or oyster—some kind of fish.

2. Fish (read back)
"It doesn't look like a fish to me anymore. It looks like what I said before."

3. Well, something is being pulled apart, some destruction or other —it could be—like someone maybe being pulled apart. Some conflict.

3. "Some kind of conflict. Two destroying agencies pulling some object apart.
Q. (Describe) "Well, it might be a woman and those two agencies pulling her apart could connote—denote many things." (Studies card) "I don't know what they are."
Q. (Why pulling her apart?)
"I didn't mean physically apart. I meant from the conflicts—physical conflict could be included, but that wasn't the main thing—other conflicts of the world, good and evil.
Q. (Describe the woman)
"The only reason I thought she was a woman was she has a dress on—you can see her body, the lower part of her body, and also, the upper part of the body is built more like a woman."
Q. (No other parts to point out.)

II. 2″

1. Two clowns—(laughs)—"Maybe the two clowns are having an argument or something, or maybe clapping hands."
Maybe they're two actors dressed in some kind of costumes.

1. "Yes, I think they're two clowns putting on a show, and they're laughing —more laughing than putting on a show, and they're clapping hands."
Q. Clowns because the red faces somehow give you the impression—at least the color in the faces there—don't know what it is—open mouths—could be laughing.

III. 2″

1. A couple of natives pounding drums. (Turns card, then turns back) "You could spend a whole hour on one of these, couldn't you?"

1. "Yes, that's what it looks like. Just the shape of their bodies—the dark black color looks like natives—negroes."
"I can't account for anything else in that picture. Don't know what the significance is."
"Carrying water maybe."
"Don't see any connection with these three objects (red *D*s). Don't know what they're for."

IV. 5″

1. Some kind of monster—maybe a giant.
Studies card—"About all I can think of."

1. "Yes, because of his legs—because of his big shoes—big feet."
"Don't know what that middle object can be."
"That's about all I can see."
Q. Other parts seen?
"Just his arms—maybe he lost them in a fight—or accident or something.
Q. "Because I called him a giant, but his arms are hanging down—not as big as his legs. They look like stumps to me."

V. 10″

1. Butterfly

1. "Got the legs—the feet of a butterfly (lower *d*) and you've got the upper part of body up here (vaguely upper *d*) and these are his wings."
Q. Dancer?

2. Maybe it's a dancer.

2. "Yes, I just see her feet—don't know what this could be unless it's her costume—a lady dancer. Sometimes they have all that stuff hanging around, swinging around."
Q. "Dancer because of the small legs."
"I don't see her feet, so it looks like she might be a ballerina. She is up on her toes."
Q. "Yes W. That's her upper body (upper *d*)—these are her legs and her costume and she's swinging around."
Q. (What upper *d* is)
"Gee, I don't know. Maybe it's the hat she has on. You can't see her face."

3. "Two forces coming together—denotes some kind of conflict." (points to lower side *ds*)

3. "Yes, it looks like two forces because of the way it's up like this—it looks like they're using their power. It's the way two people would push, or any kind of forces. It's gradual." Q. "They don't come right together; it's gradual."

Q. Location?

"Oh, this is the main body here and here (usual wings). I don't know what this is; a)—it looks like two faces, maybe two people are kissing. I don't know."

Q. "Here and here. It looks like two people are kissing." Q. "I guess they are one man and one woman—don't know." Q. "No, doesn't matter which is which."

VI. 7"

1. "Looks like an Indian sitting down on a big chair. We're seeing the back of the Indian—sitting on his throne."

1. "That looks like his body—small shoulders; that definitely looks like the back of an Indian's head and this looks like the chair—his throne."

Q. Sitting?

"You can see how stiff and straight he holds himself—like the chief would."

Q. Indian?

"The feathers here."

VII. 10"

1. "Like bookends to me. Their faces are dogs'—the wood ends—the wood ends are dogs—paws here and their faces looking at each other."

1. "Yes, these are the faces and these their paws." Q. "Bookends because it's not rounded like a dog—it looks so rock-like—like a statue."

Q. Lower *D* in picture?

"That might be the bottom of the bookend." The dogs are on here. Don't know what those two things on top are (upper *d*).

Q. "Dogs because—I guess I'm thinking of a particular type of dog—the face of it—small ones—don't know the name. They're real small and black, or red, don't know what they are—not spaniels. You don't see many around any more."

VIII. 12″

1. "They look like two rats—devouring—eating something decaying."

    1. "Yes, they look like the rats (points) and they've got their arms and legs on this. Don't know what it could be—some kind of food or it could be a trap."

    Q. "Arms and legs of the rats."

    Q. Trap upper two *D*s.

    Q. "It's built like a vine or leaves—it's loose—there're holes in it."

    Q. "I don't see anything caught in there: it looks like there *should* be something caught, but I don't see anything."

IX. 5″

1. "Two witches fishing on rocks—I guess. They're sitting on rocks." (long pause)

    1. "These are the witches (upper *D*s) and the pointed objects look like the tops of the heads of the witches. These look like the fishing rods."

    Q. (Top of heads?)

    "Right up here." (points)

2. "Maybe these are different steps to success. The first step is stagnant—no life there at all.

The second step—there's some life there. It's either trying to push you off the first step, or is holding up the first step.

The first step—there's either a conflict between the two denotations up there—or there's—they're getting along—they're happy—they're efficient, or amiable.

    2. First step (lower red D)

    Q. Stagnant because no life. Here you have things protruding (green area pointed to) you have definite objects.

    Q. Steps to success because there is—right in here you have either a pushing or a pulling or a yanking or something that denotes action of some kind.

    Trying to pull himself up to the other guys or yank the other guys down—or—

    They could be sittting down with their arms or hands like that—(demonstrates with own hands).

    Q. (Why either conflict or getting along etc.?)

    "Well, there's no conflict. They're separated."

    Q. One is over here and one is over here (upper Ds)

    "In the other pictures (all the 8 cards) the objects are close together."

X. 29″

"Gee I don't know what this is!"

50″

1. "Maybe it is a person trying to be free—but first of all he has all these different attachments.

Maybe it is to another person (the attachment) or humanity as a whole.

Then he has all the different material objects holding him down.

I'm breaking this up into two people and there are two connections—one on bottom and one on top. I'm talking now of one person and the connection is to humanity—and that could be included in many ways. (Long pause.)

He would be limited in his knowledge. See this pipe up here —that shows me that he's limited by knowledge—he's so very limited.

Then there is the connection with the flesh—sex.

And these other objects around denote material goods of the world, such as drinking—and the best things of life; I mean, material things."

1. Q. (Two pink areas the people.)

Q. (Describe?)

"Well this is the attachment I spoke of—the attachment of their natures. It's not two persons. This is one person and this—the rest of mankind."

Q. (Right red area the one person.)

Q. (Left area the rest of mankind.)

Q. "Either one could be the one trying to get free and the other, the rest of mankind. Either could represent the limitedness of man."

Q. (Upper *D* the connections on top.) (Usual "blue birds" the one on bottom.)

Q. Parts of person seen?

"This is his body, this (in upper grey *D*) his head—that's as far as I can go. These other parts I'd say—the connection of man to man—it's limited. That seems to be stronger than the inclinations of the flesh which is down below."

Q. "Stronger because it's on top."

Q. (Usual blue birds?) The flesh— sex. Q. "Because there is a connection between them and because the connection is down there where normally the sexual organs would be—of a person—the stomach and below."

Q. "These (Side Ds) are the connection with the flesh. Adds, "That (usual wishbone) could be gold right there. It looks like gold. Q. Gold because it looks like some kind of bracelet or trimming or trinket."

Q. "Material things because there's something definite here. You can point your finger at it—and yet they are not directly connected. They're attachments."

E. *Rorschach Evaluation**

The most immediate impression one gains from this Rorschach is that of acute (subjectively experienced) discomfort. There is no doubt that the patient feels himself in the throes of intense conflict, with marked anxiety and guilt reactions. There is a deeply obsessive aspect to this conflict, as though he cannot give up certain thoughts or ideas, even though dwelling on them in this ruminative way is painful and unpleasant; alien to the kind of thinking he *wants* to engage in. It also seems clear that, not only is he a prey to these ego-alien thoughts; he is also victimized because, not being able to accept his own aggression, he has, perforce, turned these feelings against himself. When these "angers" reach their peak, he reacts with feelings of inferiority and ineffectiveness.

It is evident, however, that these moods of self-belittlement have not culminated in a constant or heavy depression. The picture has a lability suggestive of mood swings. Seemingly there are recurring moments in which the ego asserts its right to self-esteem, and during which these disphoric ideas are dispelled. In their place comes a sense of ego-expansion (with all the hopefulness characteristic of this feeling). At these moments he strains for fulfillment and ego satisfaction. Under the impact of these feelings, tender reactions are projected onto the environment. The world becomes a good place; peopled with human beings to whom he would like to "give" (as we may hypothesize, some time in his past, he also received). It seems clear, however, that anxiety breaks in, unsettling these upstanding self-attitudes. The fear of a renewal of the compulsive "bad thoughts" carries with it an awareness of the bad mingled with the good; taking on the form of compulsive doubting. The uncertainty about values and their constancy now becomes a trap in which insecurity and fear imprison him so closely that they gradually encroach upon the positive self-concept, until finally it seems to him that this ambivalent, indecisive individual is his *real* self. At such periods we can fancy that despair takes over; he sees

---

* The procedures followed here are described by Klopfer *et al*, in Volumes I & II of Development in the Rorschach Technique. (12) (13)

himself as very sick; entirely dependent on some rescuing "other person."

This brings us to a second level of interpretation. Here we must search beneath this "immediate impression" (the symptom picture as the patient experiences it) and ask ourselves the same questions answered so negatively by him in his moments of panic. How sick actually is this patient? As we read the Rorschach responses (particularly those in Cards IX and X) the question of a possible psychosis must rise to the interpreter's mind. The differentiation between depth and intensity of disturbance is relevant at this point. There is no doubt about the intensity of this patient's turmoil. Nor is there any doubt that he frequently feels himself very sick and helpless. For all the turmoil, however, the Rorschach present a viewpoint which, in the main, is reassuring; answering the problem of differential diagnosis in terms of an acute anxiety reaction and not a psychosis.

These statements are in no way meant to deny the gnawing and enervating effect of his conflicts. They do not imply that either his present adjustment or his maturity level at all approximate his potential capacity. They do not cancel out his dependency needs. On the contrary, without therapeutic help it seems unlikely that either the ruminative, compulsive adaptation, or the recurrent panic states will substantially change. But there is sufficient evidence that sound ego growth has taken place, to suggest that there is a firm foundation on which to build a more stable structure. Moreover, while little actual interpersonal relating is evident in his current adaptation, the sensitiveness and empathetic reactions on which such relating depends are seen as present; dormant it is true, but not dead. Prognostically, then, there is the potentiality that they can be awakened. How this will come about, we cannot yet say. Perhaps, however, we ourselves can free-associate to the percept offered by the patient in Card V (the man and woman kissing one another).

A third level of interpretation is reached if, again looking beneath the symptom picture, we can explore the developmental implications and the psychological problems which underlie these reactions. Here the frame of reference is psychoanalytic.

The development we are concerned with on this level is his psychosexual development.

In large measure, context clues point the way. "Someone" is being pulled apart in Card I; the giant of Card IV is bereft of his powerful arms; the two opposing forces of Card V which, surprisingly, give way to a kiss between a man and a woman; the Indian Chief of Card VI sitting so that one cannot see his face; the "real small" book-end dogs of Card VII; (dogs from a remembered past, but of a kind which "you don't see around any more"); the two rats of Card VIII who, it seems, may be trapped by the very food which at first they were devouring; the "steps to success" of Card IX which culminate in the two witches, who instead of casting malevolent spells are sitting together, peacefully fishing; and last, the "person" in Card X "struggling to be free."

What do all these responses say in relation to the growing up of the little boy who has now become our patient? For one thing, they tell us that, genetically, the problems of today have a long history. Such content as food which might also be a trap (Card VIII); rats devouring the decaying matter (Card VIII); the ambivalently conceived witches (Card IX); and the person so "limited" and yet, struggling so manfully to gain freedom (Card X); all these suggest fixation and/or regression points on the various levels which actually form the "steps to success" (or failure).

Most importantly, however, these context clues point to the fact that even though there were difficulties and even some stoppages, in the main, growth and development *did* take place. The content stress in this Rorschach (as also in its qualitative aspects) is on a problem which can only become such if there is a strong and struggling ego. It is the problem of arriving at a type of masculine identification which will make his own wish for mature sexual relations possible and right, and which will free him of the guilt with which sexuality is now endowed.

Before this can take place, we may hypothesize that it will be necessary that the "Indian Chief" turn back and face the person from whom he has turned away, and that the "giant" regain his arms so that, hand in hand, he may accompany the boy up the "steps to success."

Card VII with its carved dogs suggest that the care-free play period of childhood in some way came to an early end. These are not frisking, frolicking dogs, comparable to the clowns of Card II. They are wooden. Not only did it happen long ago ("a kind of little dog not around today"); the conflict implicit in the "book-end-wood-end" confused verbalization suggests that it happened at a period when "ends" had an importance; a period roughly around the second or third year. Since the wooden dogs are in Card VII, it seems possible that the relationship to the mother (so frequently elicited by this card) was one which in some way played a part in arresting the frolic of the "little dog." (It seems noteworthy that this Subject with four *M* did not see *M* in this particular card).

In speculating about the rejecting "Indian Chief" we are led to suspect that some sense of guilt is associated for this patient with the turning away of the "chief." In some way the little boy's "badness" must have been felt to be the cause of the "chief" turning from him. It must have been a tremendous "wrong" to cause so complete a turn! However, though we may suspect an early trauma which interfered with the full establishment of masculine identification, we can assume that some partial or transient father-substitute was found, since sufficient ego growth took place that this patient is currently able to struggle toward an adult love relationship. (Serene above the conflict, and a little remote from it, are the "man and woman" of Card V "kissing").

The problem, then, seems primarily one of enabling this young man to reduce guilt to an extent where assertive masculinity can develop. The word *primarily* is used since it is not suggested that this is the *only* problem, or that, should this reduction of guilt take place, the patient will thereafter be conflict-free. As has been said, many of his problems have an infantile source, and will remain fixation points toward which, in times of stress, some regression may be expected to take place. But until relatively recently he clearly managed, in spite of these problems (W 45%; W:

M 10: 4: *D* equals 45%). The frustrated needs of young manhood seemingly then proved the stumbling block, reactivating the earlier difficulties. It is therefore felt that therapy on an ego level will suffice to restore his confidence and enable him to find satisfactions appropriate to his age and its concomitant impulses. Card X pictures an ego goal; a person "struggling to be free." Freedom, in this case, can be envisaged as joining two people in such a way that "attachment" will no longer be felt as a barrier to freedom; no longer, therefore, needing to be sublimated through "good deeds." Once it can be experienced directly; once these people *are* joined, we can even picture our patient bringing the "golden trinket" as a gift; a token of love, both personal and in the added sense of a mature, outgoing relatedness to life. Should this take place, he will no longer feel "limited by sex." Instead, he will feel fulfilled!

F. *Brief Summary of Therapy Session with above Patient*

The patient was seen in therapy by the writer for 25 sessions, distributed over a period of twelve months. Owing to the nature of the patient's particular school situation, two interruptions of three months duration were interspersed between two periods of therapy, each therapy period also lasting for three months. Two final sessions followed the second of these interruptions.

The work itself can best be thought of in terms of three phases of therapy, each phase coinciding with the three periods of time just described.

Phase I: Patient came to the clinic, self-referred, because of his panic state. The panic was verbalized as a fear that he would not be able to complete his schooling, owing to marked and growing concentration difficulties and to the discouraging effect of generalized inadequacy feelings (called by him an "inferiority complex.") The panic was so great that, after the testing was completed, an appointment was immediately made for the next day "so that we can talk about what the tests show."

This interpretative session made it clear that the patient wanted and was accessible to the kind of "exploring" help which the therapist could offer. It also made it clear that an emergency type of ego-supportive therapy was strongly indicated. The objective was to "hold the fort," so far as his schooling was concerned, and to enable patient to feel less "inferior" and inadequate. After the first two months a new and additional objective developed; that of helping the patient prepare for, and tolerate, the three month's interruption, during which his work took him to another city. The subject matter discussed centered almost entirely around his current problems in living.

The patient was able to leave in a relatively relaxed state of mind.

Phase II: This relatively relaxed state was still sufficiently operative to make it possible to shift attention from current panic reactions, to the guilt and insecurities which had manifested themselves in the previous anxiety reaction. The patient almost immediately spoke of his guilt feelings, recognizing that factually they were all out of proportion to anything "bad" he had done. Yet, he insisted, he was always feeling himself bad and unworthy; someone other people could not possibly like. He continued, "Even about my home, I was different from the other kids. The rest of them all had fathers. It made me feel queer, somehow." Therapist picked this up, observing that it might well happen to a boy as small as he had been at the time his father died, that he might feel as though his father "left him" because in some way he was "bad." This produced a number of associations from patient culminating, after several sessions, in a repetition of the account (previously given in the Structured Interview) of the time when he was "fresh" to his older brother's girl friend, and his brother had hit him. He reiterated, with an awareness of surprise at his own statement, the remembered words, "I wish you'd hit me harder, Tom, much, much harder." This opened the door to an exploration of the "guilt" which had made him feel himself so unworthy.

As part of this exploration, a small boy's developmentally appropriate "wish" to have exclusive right to his mother was considered. So also was the sense of guilt to the father which this feeling inevitably stirs up. The gradual relinquishing of this "wish" was explained, as part of a *fortunate* growth process, when, hopefully, there is an understanding (good) father. In his case there was no father, and hence a potential guilt was stirred up which could not be "worked through." Later, when the older brother hit him, the guilt became focussed (and largely displaced) into this situation, the brother becoming a sort of punishing father who, like the father of the patient's small childhood, wanted only to "turn his back on him."

The writer is aware that, stated so briefly, this sounds like a highly intellectualized explanation. It should be recalled, however, that this material took the greater part of 12 sessions to work through.*

At the last session before the second three months' break, the patient spoke of feeling ready to go to his new assignment. Seemingly, however, there was still something to be done. As he was about to leave the patient said, "Do you know, I've never asked you if you are married." He then asked, "Do you have children?" The affirmative answer, given in a word, sufficed. In saying goodbye, for the first time he did not address the therapist as "Doctor." Instead, he used the word "Mrs."

Phase III: The last phase consisted of but two interviews. The patient had come back to this city merely to graduate from his school. He was almost immediately to take a permanent assignment in another city.

He arrived 20 minutes late and, hardly pausing to greet the therapist, immediately verbalized negative feelings toward her. He felt that many of the things she had said really did not apply to him at all. He felt, besides, that he had been too dependent for awhile. Women encourage that sort of thing! He was sorry now that he had let it develop but, at least, he doesn't feel that way any more! He also indicated that, when he was settled in his new home, he was going to seek therapy with a man, and one with his own religious background.

These feelings were "accepted," but acceptance did not allay the anger. Patient slammed the door so vigorously when he left, that the therapist thought he might actually "prefer" to end on an angry note, and therefore not come to his last appointment.

---

* For a fuller description of the type of ego-supportive therapy discussed here, the reader is referred to the chapter on Principles of Corrective Emotional Experience in Psycho-Analytic Therapy (Alexander and French) 14.

When he came, his mood had changed somewhat. He "hoped" the therapist had not been too hurt at what he had said. He *did* feel friendly, but he didn't want to be tied to her apron strings!

The therapist "understood" and, of course, "respected" the way the patient felt. It was agreed, in saying goodbye, that people can be mutually friendly, and still not see eye to eye. As he left, he offered, "Perhaps I'll drop you a card once in a while to tell you how I'm getting along." The therapist smiled.

If, in part, her smile was less in farewell than in welcome to the young man who had just shouldered manhood, this seemed legitimately her secret.

Bibliography

1. Machover, Karen: *Draw-a-Person Test*. Springfield, Thomas, 1957.
2. Murray, Henry A.: *Thematic Apperception Test Manual*, Cambridge, Harvard University Printing Office, 1945.
3. Saul, Leon J.: The Psychoanalytic Diagnostic Interview, *The Psychoanalytic Quarterly, 26:* 1, 1957.
4. Buck, John J.: House-Tree-Person Test, Clinical Psychology, January 1949.
5. Gill, Neuman, and Redlich: *The Initial Interview in Psychiatric Practice*, New York, International Universities Press, Inc., 1954.
6. Whitehouse, J. C.: Guide to Interviewing and Clinical Personality study, *Archives of Neurology and Psychiatry, 52*, 1954.
7. Erikson, Erik: *Childhood and Society*, New York, W. W. Norton, 1950.
8. Schafer, Roy: *Psychoanalytic Interpretation in Rorschach Testing*, New York, Grune and Stratton, 1954.
9. Sullivan, H. S.: The Psychiatric Interview, *Psychiatry, 14:* 1951— The Psychiatric Interview, *Psychiatry, 15:* 1952.
10. Erikson, Erik: The Struggle for Ego Identity, *American Journal of Psychoanalysis*, 1955.
11. Vorhaus, Pauline G.: The Use of the Rorschach in Preventive Mental Hygiene, *Journal of Projective Techniques:* 16, 2: 1952.
12. Klopfer, Bruno, et al.: *Developments in the Rorschach Technique*, Vol. I, New York, World Book Co., 1955.
13. Klopfer, Bruno, et al.: *Developments in the Rorschach Technique*, Vol. II, New York, World Book Co., 1956.
14. Alexander, Franz and French, Thomas Morton, *Psychoanalytic Therapy*, New York, The Ronald Press Co., 1946.

INTERACTION TESTING:

A Technique for the Psychological Evaluation of Small Groups

Melvin Roman, Ph.D.
Gerald Bauman, Ph.D.

Introduction

This chapter will describe and illustrate a new psychological testing technique for small groups. Called Interaction Testing, the technique derives from a theoretical position which assumes individual-group psychological isomorphism. In essence, it is assumed that the inner psychological organization of groups is fundamentally similar to that of individuals. That is, groups can be characterized as dynamic wholes having psychological attributes of their own, including intelligence and personality. Also, the personality and intelligence of a group are emergents. They are the unique products of the interaction of its members and, therefore, cannot be deduced simply from knowledge of the personality and intelligence of its individuals.

Background

It is not uncommon in the history of science that discredited ideas are later "rediscovered" for the truths they contain. In 1920, McDougall (11) introduced the concept of "group mind" as basic to the understanding of group behavior. McDougall held that groups, like individuals, have relatively persistent interrelated characteristics which differentiate one group from others, and that it is necessary and rewarding to deal with groups as single dynamic entities.

McDougall's position was described as mystical, unscientific and generally untenable by his professional peers in American

Psychology who were, at that time, much taken with the new Behaviorism. The emergence of Gestalt Psychology, with its carefully reasoned attack on the atomistic conceptions of Behaviorism, led to significant changes in subsequent psychological thinking about groups. The Gestalt insistence and demonstration, in the field of human perception, that the whole is different than the sum of the parts, encouraged social psychologists to take a new look at groups. This "new look" ushered in a remarkably productive period in Social Psychology, epitomized by the work of Lewin (10) and his colleagues. Through their work, for example, we now know that the properties of a group such as its goals, organization and stability are in many ways significantly different from the goals, organization and stability of the individuals in the group. It is noteworthy that the choice of concepts like goals, stability and even inner psychological organization points to some leaning toward analogous thinking as between groups and individuals. Thus Lewin and his coworkers helped to establish that the group is a dynamic entity having emergent characteristics, which are not simply deducible from those of its members.

There is a discernible trend in current thinking about the nature of groups which cross-cuts such fields as sociology (6), social psychology (3), psychoanalysis (2), and political science (12), and can be described as the tendency to use the individual as a conceptual model for the study of groups. Cattell (4) offers an incisive description of a rationale for this theoretical position:

"The behavior of a group has more formal resemblance to the behavior of an individual organism than to any other natural entity, principally in the following respects:

1. A group preserves characteristic behavior habits and structure despite the continual replacement of actual individuals.

2. It shows memory for group experience and learning.

3. It is capable of responding as a whole to stimuli directed to its parts, i.e., it tends to solve problems of individuals and and sub-groups by group action.

4. It possesses drives which become more or less integrated in executive functions of nutrition, acquisition, aggression, de-

fense, etc. Groups vary in dynamic integration analogously to the variations of individuals in character.

5. It experiences "moods" of expansiveness, depression, pugnacity, . . .
6. It shows collective deliberation, a process highly analogous to the trial and error thinking of the individual. . . .

It is important to recognize that the hypothesis of individual-group psychological isomorphism in no way denies the existence of significant differences in structure between individuals and groups. It offers, rather, a conceptual approach to the study of group behavior which seems promising.

In the field of psychological testing there have been some interesting developments along these lines. The first attempt at developing a projective test for the diagnosis of group properties has been made by Horwitz and Cartwright (9). Their technique is to present a group with a relatively unstructured picture and modified T.A.T. instructions. The way the interacting group deals with the unstructured stimulus—revealed in the story the group tells about the picture—provides some insights into the group's structure and processes. Using this technique, Henry and Guetzkow (8) developed the Test of Group Projection. This is a five card T.A.T.-type test in which analysis is focused upon the final written stories of the group. The data are interpreted within an essentially social-psychological framework, with focus on such group characteristics as communication clarity, content-procedure ratio, goal concentration, role differentiation, in-group feeling, etc. Interaction Testing attempts to carry the above described efforts a step further by introducing a clinical orientation to the psychometrics of groups. In addition, Interaction Testing was originally developed with the hope that it might become a significant tool for the testing and refinement of the hypothesis of individual-group psychological isomorphism.

Interaction Testing

Procedure: Using established individual psychological tests, such as the Rorschach, T.A.T., Wechsler-Bellevue, etc., the following procedure is used.

a. Each member of the group is tested separately.

b. The group is assembled and the test (or tests) readministered with the requirement that the group-as-a-group arrive at test responses. In addition to the final product (the test protocol), the process by which the group arrives at its final responses is recorded.

Data and Treatment

1. Raw Data: Three types of raw data are elicited.

a. Test protocols of the individual members. These are scored and interpreted in the standard manner developed for the test.

b. The interaction process. The process data can be approached in a variety of ways ranging from the informal kind of clinical content analysis to such relatively formal approaches as the Bales technique for interaction analysis (1).

c. The interaction product. The test protocol obtained from the group-as-a-whole is scored and interpreted as though it had been obtained from an individual; that is, by the same rules as were applied to data in category "a" above.

2. Inferential Data: A second order of data becomes available if we compare the group product with those of the individual members. Such comparison allows the interpreter to speculate about the constructiveness of the group's use of its inner resources, that is, its members. We have found in making these comparisons between group and individual products that three concepts can encompass all of the inferred interaction processes that resulted in the group responses. The group's final response to any test item is a result of either Reinforcement, Selection, or Emergence, defined operationally as follows:

Reinforcement applies to the situation in which the group response is essentially the same as that of each member of the group when tested individually.

Selection applies to the situation in which the group response is the same as that of at least one of the individuals in the group and different from that of at least one of the individuals.

Emergence applies to the situation in which the group response is different from all of the individual responses.

These interaction categories can be characterized as either positive or negative, based on generally accepted test criteria for health and pathology. A simple example from a marriage at this point may help to illustrate how a group's responses are categorized. Let the problem be: How much is 2 plus 2? Looking at Chart 1 we see that if in individual testing, H says 3, W says 2, and together they say 4, then this is an illustration of positive emergence, since neither H nor W individually had offered the correct answer, but in interaction did. If H says 4, W says 4, and together they say 3, then this would be categorized as negative emergence, etc.

CHART 1*

INTERACTION PROCESS CATEGORIES

H	W	HWI	Category	Possible Meaning
3	2	4	positive emergence	creative interaction in healthy direction
4	4	3	negative emergence	creative interaction in unhealthy direction
4	2	4	positive selection	appropriate utilization of intra-group resources when active judgment is required
4	2	2	negative selection	inappropriate utilization of intra-group resources when active judgment is required
4	4	4	positive reinforcement	appropriate utilization of resources; mutuality in the direction of health
3	3	3	negative reinforcement	apparent absence of resources; mutual reinforcement of pathology

----

* H — husband
  W — wife
  HWI — husband and wife jointly

Before proceeding with some examples from clinical data of the various interaction categories, some comment is in order. While it appears to us that these categories can be scored reliably, their psychological meaning is not as easy to ascertain. It will surely be misleading if this scoring system is interpreted in any mechanical way, in the absence of sound clinical judgment, until some clarifying research has been done.

For example, if we look at the category of Emergence, it is apparent that there are at least three different processes which can result in a response so scored.

Emergence may be scored when:

1. The group situation has in some way reduced the threshold for the new response in one of the members. The group situation will then have made the new response more available.

2. Some test-retest effect within an individual has made the new response more available; in this case the new response would have occurred whether or not retesting had taken place in a group setting.

3. Some creative fusion has occurred among the group members resulting in a response unique to the group; not previously available to any of the individuals. This kind of situation, if it occurs at all, seems of special theoretical interest for the study of creativity in groups and individuals.

Needless to say the above considerations in some ways apply also to the categories of Reinforcement and Selection. Having noted the precautions, we will now present some illustrative data.

The clinical illustrations will be presented in the following order:

Detailed Case Studies
    A Comparison of Two Marriages
    An Engaged Couple in Conflict
    A Mother and Schizophrenic Son
Brief Case Studies
    A Stable Homosexual Relationship
    A Therapy Group at Two Points in Treatment

A Comparison of Two Marriages*

I. Psychiatric Social Worker's Interview—The Psychiatric Social Worker interviewed each couple as a couple. Her impressions are summarized here to give the reader some frame of reference regarding the "personality" of each marriage.

II. Interaction Testing—In this section we will contrast some of the data obtained from the two groups on the Wechsler-Bellevue Intelligence Scale, Form I (Comprehension, Similarities and Prorated Verbal IQ) and the Rorschach (Davidson Adjustment Scale).

III. Excerpts from "Blind" Psychological Reports.

Social Worker's Comparative Summary of Two Couples

COUPLE A	COUPLE B
DESCRIPTION: H accountant, age 40. W receptionist, age 33. Married 9 yrs. No previous marriage. No children. Fit stereotype of attractive, well-groomed business couple. Both at least average IQ. H brighter, W dominant.	H photographer, age 56. W free-lance illustrator, age 51. Married 6 yrs. Each previously married and divorced once. No children. H scrawny, wiry, tense, restless, disheveled, very bright and articulate, bizarre grimaces and verbal content. W pleasant-looking, soft-spoken, calm and gentle manner, well-organized, unusually bright and articulate, subtly odd.
COUPLE'S CONCEPT OF MARRIAGE: Both stress a good marriage to be one in which spouses do everything together and in complete agreement. Any individual difference is necessarily negative. "Marriage can't change or reduce problems, but can be better than the sum of its positives."	Both stress a good marriage to be one in which spouses can have maximum expression of individuality, with each accepting and alleviating the problems of the other.

---

* The authors are grateful to Jo Roman, M.S.S. for the collection and evaluation of interview data and to Rochelle Cohen, M.A. and Lawrence Epstein, Ph.D. for their assistance in interpreting some of the psychological test data.

VIEW OF OWN MARRIAGE:

H ". . . better than expected . . ."
W ". . . as good as expected . . ."

H ". . . magnificent fulfillment . . . untold misery . . . my cure . . . gives me strength and direction . . ."
W ". . . rewarding . . . maturing."
H and W agree it is difficult, but it is gratifying and to be preserved.

SATISFACTIONS NOTED BY COUPLE:

Achievement of their concept of an ideal and harmonious marriage. Mutual self-respect.

Expression and sharing of creative and intellectual stimulation. Sense of maturity. Relief.

CONFLICTS NOTED BY COUPLE:

None of any consequence.

Conflict pervades all areas of functioning. Can discuss readily except in reference to their essentially non-existent sexual relationship.

RELATIONSHIP AS OBSERVED BY PSW:

Couple wishes and is currently able to maintain a facade of a flawless marriage, through mutual denial of problems and restriction of individual differences, thus markedly reducing existing individuality or mutual potential for growth, and preventing dissolution of pathology. Very stable couple. Stability has detrimental characteristic of increasing rigidity, as well as positive value.

Confirm couple's own evaluation, except believe depth of pathology of both individuals is consciously somewhat underestimated—especially the pathology of wife. Though marriage is ostensibly rather chaotic, there is a kind of stability in the relationship. This seems to reflect the relief each feels in being able to maintain any kind of a relationship—especially one which accepts and allows expression of pathology.

Characteristic Dialogue: (Interviewer asks couple how they feel about marriage)

MR. & MRS. A.

H: Well, it's better than I expected. We do everything together and get along very well. I suppose it'd be even better if I could make more money.

W: I'd say it's as good as I expected. I suppose anyone could use more money. If you have problems when you get married, it's a mistake to think the marriage could correct them. We agree on everything, and never have separate friends, so we don't have any problems.

H: Yes, we do everything together. Being together is better than being by yourself, isn't it?

W: That's right. You see, there's really nothing we don't agree on.

MR. & MRS. B.

H: It's the most wonderful and the most terrible thing that has happened to me. I'm very neurotic, and I don't know how Ruth (fictitious name for wife) can live with me. Sometimes it's so terrible I have to stay away from her. I experience the most untold misery. It's like being stuck. I feel I'm being strangled, choked, and murdered. I get violent and destructive urges. Usually I don't express them, so I wait 'til Ruth can bear it and then go. This (said with almost tearful tenderness) is my cure and brings us new closeness — magnificent fulfillment. Ruth, what do you think?

W: Yes, Bob (fictitious name for husband) is very neurotic, but we knew that when we married. It doesn't prevent me from doing my work, and it's true we do have a great closeness. We're both creative people and enjoy our discussions. We don't have to be together unless we want to be. Somehow I feel Bob has helped me mature and feel much stronger. I do feel some disappointment and sense of resignation that our marriage isn't better, but my gratification is stronger.

H: Our marriage has given me a sense of direction and feelings of new energies.

Interaction Testing

Now let us look at the material derived from testing husband and wife individually, and from having each couple produce joint responses through discussion.

Figure 1 depicts six pro-rated Wechsler-Bellevue Verbal IQ scores, three for each couple: H (husband's) IQ, W (wife's) IQ, and I (interaction) IQ.*

---

* It should be kept in mind that we are assuming that Interaction Test scores can be treated psychologically and statistically as if they had been obtained from an individual.

The following can be seen from the figure. First, all three scores for the B marriage are higher than the corresponding scores for the A marriage. In the B marriage, husband receives an IQ of 122, wife 144 plus, and the B marriage an IQ of 133. In the A marriage, husband achieves an IQ of 112, wife 101, and the A marriage an IQ of 122.

Comparison of these data suggests that these two marriages differ markedly from each other. The A marriage is significantly brighter than its brighter member. Whereas, the B marriage is significantly less bright than its brighter member. This suggests that marriage B makes relatively poor use of the intellectual resources of its members, while the opposite seems true in the A marriage.

	Husband	Wife	Interaction
Marriage A	112	101	122
Marriage B	122	144+	133

Fig. I—W-B Prorated Verbal IQ.

Figure II depicts scores from the Comprehension sub-test on the Wechsler-Bellevue. The patterns noted above for *Figure I* are seen to recur here: that is, while the B marriage appears to have a higher degree of "social awareness" than the A marriage, marriage B functions somewhat less effectively in this area than its more effective member and the "social awareness" of marriage A appears to surpass that of either of its members.

	Husband	Wife	Interaction
Marriage A	9	8	10
Marriage B	11	17	15

Fig. II—W-B Comprehension.

Figure III depicts scores from the Similarities subtest of the Wechsler-Bellevue. Marriage A appears, for the first time, to be superior to marriage B, although its individual members continue to obtain lower or no better than equal scores than the members of marriage B. This is a somewhat dramatic finding, although not completely unexpected in view of the differences in the kinds of pathology of the two marriages. The fact that marriage A is superior to B, in logical thinking, even though its members are

much less intelligent, suggests on the one hand the degree of
pathological interaction in the B marriage or, on the other hand,
the degree of healthy interaction in the A marriage in this area.

	Husband	*Wife*	*Interaction*
Marriage A	14	11	16
Marriage B	14	17	14

Fig. III—W-B Similarities.

Summarizing this quantitative data on the intelligence of the
two couples, we have indications that marriage B is both brighter
and more disturbed than marriage A.

Figure IV further documents our impressions that marriage B
is less healthy than marriage A. It presents the Davidson Rorschach Adjustment Scores (5) for the husbands, wives and marriages. In this scale, the higher scores signify better adjustment.
Scores can range from 0 to 17.

In the A marriage the scores obtained are: H 7, W 7, I 13. For
the B's we find H 5, W 6, I 4. Here again we see evidence that
the interaction between the A's is probably significantly healthier
than the B's interaction. Further, we see evidence that Mr. and
Mrs. A individually are probably healthier than the members of
marriage B.

Until now, we have been considering the products of the interaction between husband and wife. Let us now turn to the actual
interaction process from which the personality and intelligence
of each marriage emerges.

	Husband	*Wife*	*Interaction*
Marriage A	7	7	13
Marriage B	5	6	4

Fig. IV—Davidson Rorschach Adjustment* Scale

Figure V summarizes the interaction analysis in the Comprehension subtest of the Wechsler-Bellevue. We can see that in
areas of "social awareness" there is an over-all similarity in inter-

---

* On this scale the higher scores suggest better adjustment. Scale consists of 17
adjustment signs.

action process with the B's manifesting 80% positive interaction, while the A's show 70%.

Although we do not as yet have adequate data, our experience so far suggests that the mere presence of NE (Negative emergence) in the B's record and its absence in the A's may alone be diagnostic of severe pathology in the B's marriage and of relative health in the A's marriage.

	PE	PS	PR	NE	NS	NR
Marriage A	0	5	2	0	1	2
Marriage B	1	2	5	1	1	0

Fig. V—Comprehension—Interaction Analysis*

* KEY: PE   positive emergence   NE   negative emergence
        PS   postive selection   NS   negative selection
        PR   positive reinforcement   NR   negative reinforcement

To deepen our insight into the nature of these marriages, it can be very useful to direct our attention to instances of negative interaction. For example, the most accurate response to the Comprehension test question, "Why does the state require people to get a license in order to be married?" is "For records." The B's in interaction answered, ". . . the family is regarded as the basic institution of society . . . the government insists on regulating and sustaining . . ." This is a zero response. Qualitatively, it suggests that this marriage is anxious about its own self-sustaining properties and feels a need for external regulation and support. Furthermore, the response is suggestive of an over-ideational process utilizing projective defenses.

How did Mr. and Mrs. B arrive at this response? In the individual testing, Mr. B responded with ". . . family is basis of society . . ." This is a zero response. Mrs. B said ". . . for the purposes of record . . ." This is the correct response. However, in discussion of this item, she became convinced of the correctness of Mr. B's position regarding the government's insistence on regulating and sustaining marriages. Thus, we find an example of Negative Selection, with this couple together choosing a pathological response. We know this is not simply a matter of Mrs. B submitting to Mr. B, since elsewhere in the process record she strongly and successfully maintained her own position. Rather, this response appears to reflect the healthier partner's inability to cope with the pathology of the sicker partner, possibly because in this particular area his manifest pathology activates her latent pathology.* As a result, then, their fundamental motivational similarity in this area has been revealed.

How did the A's deal with this question? In interaction both agreed that a license is required ". . . in order to prevent promiscuity," an incorrect response, reflecting this couple's preoccupation with the danger of sexual acting out, and the wish for external regulation. It expresses the repressive emphasis of the marriage and suggests a rather adolescent quality specifically in terms of sexual immaturity.

It is of interest that the individual responses of both Mr. and Mrs. A were the same as their interaction response, an example of Negative Reinforcement. In attempting to arrive at a joint response, they produced and immediately rejected the correct answer. It would appear that they equally need to deny reality in order to maintain their fantasy that marriage has resolved their individual problems. Thus we see a reality distortion based on the reinforcement of the defense mechanism of denial.

Let us now turn to the interaction analysis of the Similarities subtest. In *Figure VI* we see that the B's produce two Negative Emergence responses, while the A's produce none. As we said earlier, there is reason to believe that emergence responses—either negative or positive—are much more likely to point to the uniqueness of a given marriage. Further, the presence of two Negative Emergence responses in the B marriage with none in the A's again points to the probable presence of less pathology in the A marriage than in the B marriage.

The following is an example of Negative Emergence taken from the data of the B marriage. In response to one of the questions, both H and W individually had the right answers, but in discussion became so obsessively concerned about minor details as to be unable to agree on a response. After much heated discussion

---

* It is possible that this order of data will enable us to operationally (testwise) research the problem of complementary neuroses in marriage as described by Mittelman and others.

they agreed that they could not agree and, therefore, could not produce a joint response. It appeared as though their intellectual "paralysis" (and/or non-productivity) was in part due to their inability to relinquish the sado-masochistic gratifications inherent in their disagreement.

	PE	PS	PR	NE	NS	NR
Marriage A	2	3	6	0	0	1
Marriage B	0	2	8	2	0	0

Fig. VI—Similarities—Interaction Analysis

Figure VII helps to demonstrate the differences in the emotional life of the two marriages. This table, based on the Davidson Rorschach Adjustment Scale, demonstrates how interaction process analysis may be applied to the Rorschach data. In comparing the marriage, it is apparent that there is significantly greater healthy interaction in the A marriage than in the B marriage.

Furthermore, the degree of positive selection in the A marriage suggests that we are dealing with basically different personalities who in interaction generally tend to be sensitive to and supportive of their individual strengths. In contrast to the A's, the dominant interaction process in the B marriage is that of Negative Reinforcement. This suggests that we are dealing with basically similar personalities who in interaction generally tend to reinforce their individual pathology.

	PE	PS	PR	NE	NS	NR
Marriage A	2	9	2	0	1	1
Marriage B	0	1	3	1	2	8

Fig. VII—Davidson Adjustment Signs—Interaction Analysis

In the preceding discussion we have shown some of the ways in which data derived from Interaction Testing can be quantitatively and qualitatively treated. It is also possible to write traditional kinds of psychological reports based on Interaction Test data; i.e., to describe the personality characteristics of the group as if it were an individual. In order to demonstrate this, we asked two clinical psychologists to write so-called "blind reports" based only on the interaction data. That is, these clinicians were

DAVIDSON
RORSCHACH ADJUSTMENT SIGNS

	Marriage A			Marriage B		
	H	W	HWI	H	W	HWI
1. M greater than FM or M equal to FM				X		X
2. 3 or more M (including Addit.)		X	X	X	X	X
3. Sum C more than Fc + c + C′		X	X	X	X	X
4. F % between 30 and 50		X	X			
5. Dd + 5%, 10 or less	X	X	X	X	X	X
6. 4 or more P (les than 30% R)	X		X		X	
7. R between 20 and 40						
8. FC more than CF or FC equals CF	X		X			
9. 2 or more FC			X			
10. No Pure C	X					
11. % R for VIII, IX, X between 35-60						
12. FK + Fc 2 or more	X		X		X	
13. W : M equals approx. 2 : 1			X			
14. A % 50 or less		X	X			
15. No color shock	X		X			
16. No shading shock	X	X	X			
17. No Refusals		X	X	X	X	
Total No. Signs	7	7	13	5	6	4

KEY: H husband   W wife   HWI Interaction husband-wife

told only that the data they were evaluating was derived from husband and wife discussion. They were not given any information about history of marriage or individuals, or any other relevant data. This was done essentially to explore the degree to which accurate impressions regarding the group can be derived without knowledge of history of individuals and without test data from the individuals.

The following are brief excerpts from their detailed reports:

EXCERPTS FROM "BLIND" PSYCHOLOGICAL REPORT ON MR. AND MRS. A

"This couple by dint of considerable self-restraint and their oblique approach to one another effect a surface harmony. Yet, there is little evidence of constructive fusion of individual strengths, although there undoubtedly exist some. There seems to be a compounding of insecurities and anxieties . . . stifling growth and intensifying feelings of guilt, inadequacy and loneliness . . . they tend to avoid and deny problems in order to maintain the status quo . . . marriage tends to inhibit the expression of their separate individualities . . . yet something better seems possible. There is constructive fantasy and capacity for insight and introspection . . . the ego strength of the marriage is better than either believes it to be . . . they seem to be unaware that something is very wrong or that something better is possible . . . I think they could be rapidly awakened through counseling as a couple . . . major foci of resistance will be their use of mechanisms of denial, externalization and projection."

EXCERPTS FROM "BLIND" PSYCHOLOGICAL REPORT ON MR. AND MRS. B

"Outstanding in the Rorschach material of this marriage is the preponderance of sado-masochistic trends, themes of violence and fear, tremendous tension . . . the struggle for survival. This is a highly conflict-ridden, schizoid marriage with marked paranoid ideation . . . data suggest impaired reality testing and severe underlying depression.

"On the positive side, it should be noted that . . . there is good recoverability from the disruptive effects of conflict . . . reality testing improves when they are confronting more structured, less emotionally tinged situations . . . they are extremely intelligent and despite somewhat overwhelming tension and conflict are very often quite creative."

An Engaged Couple in Conflict

Background

Miss X and Mr. Y were referred for Interaction Testing by their psychotherapist, for an evaluation of each and of their relationship.

The main problems at the time of referral were related to their inability to make a decision about marriage. Mounting strain in the relationship seemed to be associated with their inability to move in any direction, either toward marriage or separation. Miss X and Mr. Y are professional people, in their late 20's, of middle class background.

Tests Administered

The tests administered, both individually and in interaction, were

1) Wechsler-Bellevue, Form I. (Comprehension and Similarities)

2) Rorschach—Each subject was instructed to write his responses, and to locate them, in the "Group Rorschach Blank."*

3) Figure Drawings. Each subject drew a person, then a couple. A carbon copy of each drawing was submitted to the other subject with instructions, "Change this drawing in any way that you like." These modified drawings seem to reveal more graphically than elsewhere several aspects of their attitudes toward each other and the relationship, and their reactions to these attitudes.

4) TAT. Each subject wrote his story to cards 4, 12 M and 13 MF; then the couple wrote its story. All of these stories were written at home, and mailed in.

Test Data

1) W-B. Comprehension and Similarities

	Comp	Simil.	Pro-rated Verbal I.Q.
He	14	14	128
She	18	18	144+
They	16	16	140

Items of special interest: three items elicited negative interaction:

Comprehension: Why Should We Keep Away From Bad Company?

		Score
He: Because it makes for a disagreeable evening, boring.		0
She: Because they might influence you negatively.		2
Together: Argue over the use of *bad* in the question . . . she submits to his interpretation of question . . . "like last evening" . . . They decide to choose his original response. Zero score . . . negative selection.		0

---

* Arranged by M. R. Harrower, Obtainable from the Psychological Corporation.

Similarities: In What Way Are Egg and Seed the Same?

He: Both are means of reproduction.   1

She: Both give rise to life.   2

Together: Methods of reproduction . . . he insists they are representative of means . . . and that is the more pointed similarity. Negative Selection.   1

In What Way Are Praise and Punishment the Same?

He: Both can influence a person's happiness.   0

She: Both are forms of criticism and motivation.   2

Together: Can't agree on response . . . decide to skip item . . . Negative Emergence.   0

Rorschach

CARD I

He: Gives me the impression of an uncircumcised penis.
Has the appearance of some of the parasites I studied in school (head of the parasite).

She: An insect with 2 small antennae.
A bat with wings outspread.
The body of a woman without head or legs.

They: Uncircumcised penis.
Whole thing looks like an insect.

CARD II

He: The total picture is that of 2 prehistoric or out of space creatures engaged either in some game of sport, or combat or perhaps even a dance.

She: 2 elephants facing each other with trunks touching—probably fighting and red color suggests blood.

They: 2 prehistoric creatures or elephants engaged in combat (see blood) or in a game or a dance.

CARD III

He: The total picture is that of 2 African natives carrying a basket between them.

She: 2 African native women with their hands in a cauldron probably cooking dinner. The red spots represent autumn foliage since they are out doors.

They: 2 female African natives either carrying a basket between them or cooking in a cauldron with autumn foliage in background.
Looks like female human pelvis.

CARD IV

He: The total picture of a man lying on his back with his feet toward you and a huge penis between his legs. He is also exhausted.

Looks like the labia of the vagina.

She: It looks like the pelt of an animal as seen from above.

An ape-like creature with huge feet and thin-twisted arms and a small head—(as seen from the back).

They: Total picture is that of an ape or other humanoid creature lying on its back with a huge penis between legs.

Looks like labia of a vagina.

CARD V

He: The whole picture bears a striking resemblance to a gliding bat.

She: A bat with long antennae, outspread wings.

A woman wearing a Spanish costume with huge sleeves and a headdress with 2 feathers.

They: Whole picture looks like a bat with huge wings extended.

CARD VI

He: This one looks like a darning needle (insect) as far as the black cylindrical part is concerned—the muddy shading on either side looks like mud that the insect is caught in.

She: An animal skin with a stripe down the back.

They: Black part looks like darning needle and muddy stuff on each side looks like mud that it's stuck in.

Looks like pelt or skin of an animal stretched out with a stripe down the middle.

CARD VII

He: Looks like 2 small French poodles facing each other.

Looks like 2 odd looking fish that are kissing each other.

She: A group of islands enclosing a lagoon.

Profiles of 2 women with upswept hair.

They: Looks like 2 small French poodles.

Whole thing looks like group of islands surrounding a lagoon.

. CARD VIII

He: Look exactly like wharf rats.

She: 2 mice climbing.

They: 2 wharf rats or mice climbing.

CARD IX

He: Looks like an apple.

Looks like 2 men with pointed heads fencing.

She: Areas of land and sea, the top orange part looks like coastline.

They: Looks like an apple.

2 mooseheads facing each other.

MISS X
(Age 6)

1.   MISS X — MODIFICATION BY MR Y   1a.

DRAW A PERSON

DRAW A PERSON

MISS X — MODIFICATION BY MR. Y

MISS X   2.   MISS X — MODIFICATION BY MR. Y   2a.

Psychiatric Testing Machine

DRAW A COUPLE

DRAW A COUPLE

CARD X

He: Looks like the base of the mast of a sailing ship.
          Looks like 2 fetuses in uteri attached to 2 placentas.
          Looks like a spider.

She: A garden with different colored flowers; the grey part on top looks like a piece of statuary near the entrance.
          Lobsters or crabs.
          Looks something like a grasshopper or snail.

They: Base of mast of sailing vessel.
          Crab or spider.
          Tadpole or seahorse.

DRAW A PERSON

DRAW A PERSON

DRAW A COUPLE

DRAW A COUPLE

T.A.T. Stories

CARD 12 M

He: The man lying on the couch is in a hypnotic trance into which he has been cast by the man standing over him. There is something gloomy and sinister about the whole picture so that one gets the feeling that this is almost like something out of a horror movie and that the hypnotist may be a vampire or a mad scientist who wishes to convert the man on the couch into a monster but he must first bring him under his spell. The scientist met this man at a party several days before and befriended him with the intent of luring him to his home.

She: The boy lying on the couch is the old man's grandson. Years ago, his parents died and the grandfather has raised him since he was a young child. Recently, the boy has been ill and the grandfather has given him much love and care. In the picture, the boy has finally fallen into a peaceful sleep; the crisis in his illness is over. The grandfather has just been stroking his hair fondly before leaving the room.
He will recover completely.

They: The man standing over the couch is a famous hypnotist at a party who has just been asked to give a demonstration. This boy has volunteered and has just been put to sleep. He'll make him go through various tests to prove he is really hypnotized and then will awaken him and he'll feel refreshed and wide awake.

CARD 13 MF

He: The man in this picture is very emotionally disturbed. He met the girl at a party and after taking her home he made sexual advances which were rejected. At this time he could no longer resist his impulses and raped her. He is now experiencing great guilt and shame over what he has done and will probably try to run away but will be caught and sent to prison.

She: The two young people in this picture are students who have been having an affair. They care for each other very much and have had great diffi-culty in restraining themselves from having intercourse, although the girl has very severe heart disease and has been warned against this by her doctor. In the picture they have had relations, and the young man after getting dressed and preparing to leave turns to find his girl has suddenly died. He is overcome with grief and guilt for his part in bringing this about, and it will take him many years of therapy to re-cover from the trauma.

They: This man has just come home. He called for his wife and when she did not answer he entered the bedroom and found her dead and obviously assaulted sexually. He is grief stricken and shocked. He will spend years in grief and unable to enter into a relationship with a woman because it rekindles the horror of the situation. Ultimately though, he marries again and is happy.

CARD 4

> *He:* The man in this picture has just lost his job and has depleted his finances. He feels hopeless about his future and does not know where to turn. His wife is trying to reassure him and make him understand that all is not as bleak as it may seem and that he should keep trying. Things will remain difficult for awhile but ultimately his luck will turn and he will find work again.
>
> *She:* This scene takes place in the woman's home; a rather shabby frame house "on the wrong side of the tracks." She's crazy about the virile and exciting looking man—pleading with him not to leave her. He goes for her also, but is dead broke and has had a very deprived childhood. Consequently, he is fired with ambition to travel, to learn, to make a great deal of money and he is unwilling to be saddled with a wife at this point in his life. He does leave, goes to sea and eventually does manage to attain some measure of success. During these years however, they grow far apart in their needs and wants in life and end up by marrying other people.
>
> *They:* The scene takes place in a bar and grill by the waterfront where this girl works. She is in love with the man and is begging him to stay and marry her. He loves her too but is torn between his love for freedom and the open sea to which he wants to return. He goes back to sea but finds that his love for her is stronger than anything and ultimately returns and they live together happily.

Psychological Report

Test Behavior

Individually, there was a marked contrast between the behavior of the two testees. Miss X was extremely tense and apprehensive, and was able to express this directly to the examiners. In spite of this discomfort, she was cooperative and produced what appears to be valid data in individual testing.

Mr. Y appeared to be relatively comfortable throughout testing. When mildly anxious, he would tend to engage in rather dependent, approval seeking behavior directed to the examiners. His individual protocols likewise appear to represent valid aspects of himself.

In interaction testing, there was a distinct tendency for Miss X to defer to Mr. Y. In part, this appeared to be based on embarrassment about overt discussion of differences in the presence of strangers. Because of the above she appeared to be reluctant to enter into conflict-contact with him. Mr. X, for his part, seemed not at all disturbed by this mode of interaction, appearing to accept her deference as his due. This may be an example of unconscious collusion which for him maintains the illusion that he is involved when in fact he may be detached.

In order to evaluate this pattern of interaction, two variations in testing technique were introduced. For some of the interaction protocols, the examiners left the room. For others, the clients were asked to do the interaction tests at home. The data derived from these three situations seemed to have basic consistency, to be described below, that does not appear to be a function of interacting before strangers, and is therefore likely to be highly significant.

Findings

Miss X. On the Wechsler-Bellevue Scale, she obtains a pro-rated Verbal I.Q. of 144, which is at the Very Superior level. Her test achievement is consistent and practically perfect, suggesting that besides being very gifted intellectually, her intellectual functioning as tested seems unimpaired. This finding contrasts sharply with Miss X's strong doubt and anxiety about her ability. It also indicates something of her capacity to function under stress.

Projective material suggests a diagnosis of mixed neurosis having obsessional, hysterical and narcissistic features. The test data do not suggest the presence of underlying anxiety parallel to the overt anxiety that she manifests. As in the Wechsler, we find in the projectives that Miss X make relatively good use of her creative and integrative trends.

Her self-concept, however, is extremely negative. She sees herself as a castrated, helpless, unworthy little girl who is very angry and resentful and unable to give warmth or affection. In reaction to this, she has developed a compensatory role for herself as an exhibitionistic, aggressive, exaggeratedly self-sufficient woman. Her focal concern is apparently with control. Self-derogation, withdrawal, repression, doubting and detachment apparently relate to her underlying rage, fear of its breakthrough and anticipated loss of dependent gratification. Strong masochistic trends related to guilt are prominent. Projective material contains significant data relating to problems of urethral control ("fear of soiling") suggesting pre-oedipal determinants of her sexual difficulties.

It appears that at this stage in this woman's development, her needs for synthesis are more pressing than her needs for analysis. In support of this contention, we find, first of all, very little evidence of active disorganizing pathology. Secondly, there is much evidence of a readiness for relatedness, of potential sexual and emotional warmth that are close to the surface. It would seem then that the critical current problem is the discrepancy between her concept of herself (with its correlated and sustaining provocative behavior) and her genuine capacity for relatedness, which she tries to bar from awareness. It is significant that she appears to be in a positive transference and has considerable therapeutic optimism.

Mr. Y. On the Wechsler-Bellevue, Mr. Y obtains a pro-rated Verbal I.Q. of 128, at the Very Superior level. Marked intratest variability indicates significant emotional interference with intellectual functioning. There is evidence of somewhat impaired judgment based on an overly personalized approach and sporadic impulsiveness.

Projective material is suggestive of a borderline individual with a fairly effective social facade, but with considerable underlying disturbance.

He evidences weak defensive structure, characterized by excessive use of the rather primitive defenses of projection and denial, a marked regressive pull, and intermittent loosening of reality ties under the impact of strong affective and sexual stimulation. It seems particularly important to note that despite the strong regressive trends, these are spontaneously checked and fairly good recoverability is manifested.

There is a good deal of inappropriateness, confusion, remoteness and rather primitive symbolization engendered by an omnipresent castration anxiety. Under its pressure, he regresses to a primitive oral incorporative orientation. The archaic, symbiotic aspects of this regression are most clearly revealed in the first two responses to the Rorschach, on card I: An uncircumcized penis;

head of a parasite. It must be pointed out that not all the orality is of a passive, sucking nature, since underneath the passive, seductive facade there is a good deal of oral and anal aggressiveness.

In the main, this is a man who has an extremely passive self image. He is guilt-laden, feels dirty, depressed, evidences feelings of depletion and immobilization and generally finds the masculine role to be frightening and only gratifying in adolescent-type compensatory fantasy. The homosexual potential and the possibility of anal and oral perversions are noteworthy. Another significant finding is the presence of strong voyeuristic conflict.

Interpersonally, he is essentially detached and remote, evidencing little capacity for genuine affective involvement. He has a boyish blandness and charm which probably serves him well in social and professional situations. However, the absence of a more positive affective potential in addition to the relatively superficial self-awareness suggest a course of treatment that will probably be of long duration and should be focussed on the strengthening of defenses.

Interaction

Miss X and Mr. Y. On the Wechsler-Bellevue, the pro-rated Interaction Verbal I.Q. is 140, at the Very Superior level. This performance is significantly below the group potential which is at least at Miss X's level. It is also significantly higher than Mr. Y's performance. The intellectual impairment is based on Negative Selection; essentialy this occurs through their frequent rejection of her superior answers in favor of his inferior ones. It was apparent in their test behavior as well as in their test results that this is a manifestation of their mutual misperceptions of each other: that is, their belief that he is the brighter and healthier of the two.

This mode of Negative Selection is found to be maintained through the projective material. The Rorschach protocol is found to contain a simple mixture, almost alternately, of her responses and his. Its most striking characteristic is the absence of signs that they affect each other through any real modification of responses. Essential detachment and lack of contact between them seem to be the most striking aspects of the interaction protocol.

There are noteworthy exceptions. Of the 17 responses in the Interaction Rorschach, 15 developed through selection, (about half of them negative). The other two responses are instances of Negative Emergence. This suggests that, in the rare instances of genuine contact between the two, the result is decreased effectiveness. An examination of these two instances suggests further that this genuine contact occurs on the rare occasions when Miss X is more threatened or less competent than Mr. Y, and that the interaction product is esentially a regression from his better response.

The goal of this group, as all groups, is to maintain itself. Survival of the group in this case depends upon isolation of the members and the avoidance of change. In essence, they tacitly agree not to modify one another. The Negative Emergence may then be a manifestation of the group's attempt to maintain the status quo. In essence, we see this as a fight-flight pairing designed to avoid awareness of the basic lack of contact between the members.

The motivational complementarity that maintains this relationship may be considered at several levels.

His castration anxiety with its attendant passivity and implied impotence may interlock with her fear of loss of control and frigidity, relating to her fear of her rage toward men.

The absence of real emotional contact between them appears as a defense against the stimulation of anxiety mentioned above.

The group "delusion" that she is sicker and less intelligent than he, is seen as being in the service of these needs. It limits his fear of being destroyed by a woman and her fear of destroying a man. In essence, it may serve to deny the reality that she can hurt him.

Another level of complementarity seemingly relates to his oral dependent needs for a symbiotic child-mother relationship and her acceptance of this as a way of avoiding oedipal anxieties and also of gratifying her unresolved dependency problems through identification with him.

A Mother and Son

Background

The subjects in this study were a hospitalized 19 year old schizophrenic male, having had one year of college, and his 46 year old mother, a school teacher. They are from a middle class background.

Tests Administered

1) Wechsler Adult Intelligence Scale, Comprehension and Similarities subtests.
2) Rorschach Test.

Test Data: WAIS: Significant Responses

1) WAIS: Significant Responses.

Comprehension

WHAT IS THE THING TO DO IF YOU FIND AN ENVELOPE IN THE STREET, THAT IS SEALED, AND ADDRESSED AND HAS A NEW STAMP?

Son: I'd say to deliver it if possible, or mail it, if impossible to deliver it. (1)
Mother: Mail it. (2)
Interaction: Either mail it or deliver it if addressee is close by. (1)

WHY SHOULD WE KEEP AWAY FROM BAD COMPANY?

Son: Too influential. (2)
Mother: I don't think I have an answer. I just wouldn't associate with them in the first place. People seek out their own. Actually, I don't think I ever cautioned my children to keep away from bad company. (0)
Interaction: In some cases, there is an influence, but above all, people tend to be drawn toward their own kind. (0)

WHAT SHOULD YOU DO IF WHILE IN THE MOVIES YOU WERE THE FIRST PERSON TO SEE SMOKE OR FIRE?

Son: Sound an alarm; I wouldn't start screaming "fire"; that would start a panic; I'd merely tell the usher. (2)
Mother: I'd yell "fire" and probably try to get to the nearest fire alarm box. Open the doors and perhaps see people out safely. (0)
Interaction: Notify the usher as quietly as possible. He will know what to do. (2)

WHY SHOULD PEOPLE PAY TAXES?

Son: To provide revenue for the U.S. government. (2)
Mother: It is our obligation as citizens. (0)
Interaction: To supply the government with revenue. It's the responsibility of a good citizen. (1)

WHY ARE PEOPLE WHO ARE BORN DEAF USUALLY UNABLE TO TALK?

Son: I'll have to hazard a guess. They never heard the sound of a human voice, don't know what it is, and are therefore unable to fathom that they are able to speak. (0)
Mother: Because they can't mimic sounds. (2)
Interaction: Inability to imitate. (2)

WHY DOES THE STATE REQUIRE PEOPLE TO GET A LICENSE IN ORDER TO BE MARRIED?

Son: In order to validate the marriage. I guess in order to prove that they are married. (1)

Mother: For one thing, I suppose the fee involved (laughs). Second, protection of the individual; to be sure you're not marrying a bigamist or polygamist. Also to insure permanency of the marriage. (1)

Interaction: Recorded proof of marriage. Insurance against bigamy. (1)

WHAT DOES THIS SAYING MEAN? "SHALLOW BROOKS ARE NOISY."

Son: Little people shouldn't talk big. (1)

Mother: I associate it with people. People who don't think very deeply probably are noisy to cover their shallowness. It's the opposite of "still waters run deep." (2)

Interaction: People with shallow minds make the most noise. (2)

WHAT DOES THIS SAYING MEAN? "ONE SWALLOW DOESN'T MAKE A SUMMER."

Son: I don't know, haven't the vaguest idea. (0)

Mother: You need more than one indication, more than one proof of any situation or—don't judge people by one characteristic; you need more than one proof to come to any conclusion. (2)

Interaction: A person or situation cannot be judged by one characteristic. (2)

Similarities

EYE-EAR:
Son: Both parts of the body. (1)
Mother: Senses. (2)
Interaction: Organs of sense. (2)

AIR-WATER:
Son: Both substances. (0)
Mother: Elements. (1)
Interaction: Elements. (1)

EGG-SEED:
Son: They're both seeds. They have to be fertilized in order to produce a new being. (0)
Mother: Beginning; conception. (2)
Interaction: Embryonic; beginning. (2)

POEM-STATUE:
Son: I don't see how they could be alike. (0)
Mother: Beauty. (1)
Interaction: Beauty. (1)

PRAISE-PUNISHMENT:
Son: Rewards for different kinds of behavior. (1?)
Mother: Contrast . . . both used as disciplinary measures. (2)
Interaction: It helps to alleviate guilt feelings. (0)

FLY-TREE:
Son: Both living things. (2)
Mother: I'd need an imagination for that; I suppose insects swarm around a tree. (0)
Interaction: Don't know. (0)

Rorschach Responses

CARD I

Son: A witch with four eyes.

Also something else: Mrs. Jones in Ward B.

Mother: Looks like a bird . . . Is it a bird, is it a plane, it's superman—I'd say it's a symmetrical pattern for one thing.

It's not exactly pretty. I don't like the colors at all.

Kind of a bird, a headless bird. When you look again, it's a bird in flight. Look closer, it has no head.

Interaction:

Can't agree (reject).

CARD II

Son: These look like two cardinals, doing a dance. They're the only birds I know with red heads and black bodies. Three legs. As the legs come together, there's a spurt of blood from each one.

Mother: Hmm! These faces almost look like two teddy bears . . . kissing each other.

I like those little touches of red. Sort of harmonizes with the teddies.

This looks like a butterfly down here.

The two little red designs offset the pattern.

Interaction:

Can't agree (reject).

CARD III

Son: This looks like a kind of crab. It has too few legs. And a butterfly over it.

Mother: This looks like something Dali would create; a Daliesque scene. Looks like a caricature of dancers, doing a fast dance, like those Flamenco dancers. The touches of red give it the Flamenco, done in caricature form.

That's all. Boy, you must get some weird ones, eh?

Interaction: Dancers.

CARD IV

Son: This is a worm's eye view of a three-legged giant.

Mother: This I don't like.

It looks like an ominous black cloud.

As I keep looking at it—it has no shape—just one of the cloud formations—a rain cloud—a storm cloud.

Interaction: Can't agree (reject).

CARD V

Son: This looks like the rear view of a kind of flying insect. What kind, I don't know. In fact, I don't see too much of this at all.

Mother: Another one—

It looks like a bat.

That's all; a bat in flight. I don't like the greys, you know (laughs). I like gay colors.

Interaction: Back of a bat in flight.

CARD VI

Son: A butterfly-—
Alighting on a bear rug. The bear rug has no head.

Mother: Oh, another one of these horrible greys.
Well, the symmetry in this one is very outstanding to me; the symmetrical pattern.
The top part looks like it might have a face with little whiskers; almost looks like cat's whiskers up there.
The rest is very meaningless—it looks like—the face at the end of a totem pole
Beneath that, it looks like a little wingspread.

Interaction: A combination; bear rug, totem pole, little head on top.

CARD VII

Son: This looks like two snobbish rabbits, giving each other dirty looks.

Mother: This really has a cloud-like texture.
It looks like two silhouettes—It almost looks like two little girls with pony tails up in the air.—You can't see a pony tail like that.
That's all I can see there.

Interaction: Two little girls' heads.

CARD VIII

Son: This is a couple of mountain goats climbing up an extremely rough mountain.

Mother: This looks like something out of an anatomy book—the colors are pleasant.
It looks like two bears on either side here—four-legged animals—the outside looks like two animals and—
The center part looks like—part of the spine—
But a pleasant looking formation nevertheless, even though a peculiar combination; pleasant to the eye.

Interaction: Two bears climbing on a whale's vertebrae.

CARD IX

Son: I remember this one. I have never yet been able to find anything in it—
Looks like elephants with knives through their trunks, or grasped in their trunks, riding on buffaloes.
The orange and red don't remind me of anything.

Mother: You have to look at these for awhile in order to get some kind of reaction—
This looks like a fountain—the rest reminds me of nothing—
A fountain—maybe the light creating the different colors there.

Interaction: Can't agree (reject).

CARD X

Son: This is a picture of utter confusion.

Here are two purple people-eaters with three legs apiece, fighting for possession of a pole, on top.

The green is nothing.

This is a crab with more legs than the New York Central has branch lines.

This is grasshoppers.

Caterpillars.

Yellow are scrambled eggs; right next to the red caterpillars.

Mother: This looks like Spring.

Yellow birds.

This looks like the mating season—sort of happy and carefree looking—bright, happy colors and leaves—see the leaves here, and birds—

A pair of lovers—these little animals here—This is very happy looking.

Interaction: Can't agree (reject).

Psychological Report on Interaction Testing: Son and Mother

The test behavior of the subjects was striking in several respects. They were keenly aware of the examiner, and there seemed to be a feeling in the air of a dramatic performance, enjoyed by the actors.

Soon after the testing began a quite distinct role differentiation occurred, apparently instituted by the mother. When the examiner would pose a question, she would very "school-teacherishly" turn expectantly to her son. He would give his answer, and when it differed from hers, she would question him in detail, as though using pedagogical principles to "lead him to light." In the first place, this seemed to serve her purpose of avoiding genuine mutuality in the situation; she in effect denied that she was being tested. (This was a tendency and not uniformly true throughout.) It became particularly ludicrous in situations where her son's responses were perfect and to the point, and she would try "patiently" to lead him to her own egocentric or otherwise distorted position. He felt this, and responded to it. After it had happened a few times, he tended to give his response, terminating with, "Just write that down, Mother." As we will see, this request was usually overridden, to the detriment of the final product.

One final observation about the relationship. The mother finds her son's humor very amusing, disproportionately so in the examiner's judgment. This seemed to be one part of a seductive quality in their relationship. It was manifested in many ways. One striking instance occurred when she nudged him, almost as a confidant, and made a joke at the expense of her husband. It is hard to be more specific about the qualities of this seductiveness, but it certainly seemed to be "in the air."

Table I presents the psychometric findings in the WAIS.

TABLE I. WAIS SUBTESTS AND PRO. VERBAL I.Q.

	Comprehension Scaled Score	Similarities Scaled Score	Pro-rated Verbal I.Q.
Son	13	11	114
Mother	12	13	117
Interaction	13	12	117

The table reveals that mother and son obtain essentially identical scores, and that there is no significant change when they are in interaction. Taken at face value, it suggests that the group's intellectual effectiveness has been neither enhanced nor impaired by the pairing. Since this could occur through a variety of processes, it is of interest to examine the actual details of the interaction process. (We might find, for example, that the responses of both subjects were substantially identical, so that the final product is unchanged, a result of reinforcement. If their individual responses were different in content and in adequacy, however, we would be interested in knowing what sort of "cancelling-out process" results in no net change in score.)

As we shall see, enough responses were significantly different so that it would have been possible, through Positive Selection alone, to have greatly improved their interaction score.

TABLE II WAIS INTERACTION PROCESS

	Positive						Negative					
	Reinf.		Selection		Emergence		Reinf.		Selection		Emergence	
	c	s	c	s	c	s	c	s	c	s	c	s
Individuals												
Response	o	i	o	i	o	i	o	i	o	i	o	i
Comparison	m	m	m	m	m	m	m	m	m	m	m	m
	p.	i	p.	i	p.	i	p.	i	p.	i	p.	i
		l.		l.		l.		l.		l.		l.
Son Better	–	–	1	–	–	–	–	–	3	1	–	–
Mother Better	–	–	3	4	–	–	–	–	1	–	–	1
Both Same	4	6	–	–	–	–	–	1	–	–	–	–

Table II shows us that 6 of the 14 items which elicited significantly different responses from mother and son were resolved through negative interaction. (This is consistent with our finding of no net change under interaction conditions; it suggests an overall cancellation of positive and negative interaction.)

Secondly, when the son's individual response is better, 4 out of 5 interaction processes are negative. When the mother's individual response is better, 7 out of 9 positive interactions occur. It seems consistent with this data to interpret that the mother's potential contributions through health and/or effectiveness tend to be accepted by the group, while those of the son tend to be rejected.

Combining this finding with the fact that 13 of the 14 interaction processes are Selection and not Emergence (under conditions of different response by each subject), we can infer that the group accepts the mother's dominant role indiscriminately; her responses tend to prevail.

In addition, the presence of only one Emergence response out of 14 possible ones seems to suggest a minimum of "genuine" or creative contact between the two. (Since we have no norms, we can only guess that this is really *"little"* contact.) Since the one Emergence response is Negative, we may speculate that one reason for reduced contact between the two is that it tends to be destructive when it does occur.

A summary of the findings implicit in Table II: When mother and son's WAIS responses differ in quality:

1) The interaction product results from positive interaction and negative interaction in about equal amounts, thus helping to account for no net change in group I.Q.

2) Mother plays a dominant role even when inappropriate: i.e., when son's response is more effective. Her response tends to prevail.

3) Only one Emergent response, a negative one, occurs. This suggests minimal "genuine" contact which is destructive when it does occur.

A final note on the one instance of Negative Emergence. It occurs in the Similarities item: "In what way are Praise and Punishment alike? The mother answered correctly "discipline." The son's response "reward," is inferior to his mother's but probably worthy of partial credit. Their interaction product, "to help alleviate guilt feelings" is a completely inadequate response. While it might be fruitful, we will not here speculate about the particular item that elicited one instance of Negative Emergence. It may be useful simply to describe what happened. When the son offered his response, his mother, instead of arguing, adopted the benign school-teacher role; asking him to explain further. He was some-what perplexed and she challenged him more directly to explain how punishment can be a reward. This he seemed to know inti-mately, and he readily answered that it alleviates guilt feelings. The mother was surprised and intrigued by this revelation, and accepted it as the answer to the item. The examiner felt, in this instance, that she was the prime mover in developing the poor final response, as though she had drawn out the pathology from her son. (It should be borne in mind that this view of what hap-pened is not the only possible one.)

The Rorschach material provides some interesting contrasts to the WAIS. While neither son nor mother had alone rejected any cards, in interaction they rejected five. On the whole, her Ror-schach seems significantly less disturbed than his. If we were to predict on the basis of WAIS performance, then, our guess would have been that her responses would have prevailed in Interaction Testing. Why did this fail to happen? Observation of their be-havior offers some clues. No really strong effort was made by either of them to work through to an acceptable response. They seemed to accept with relief the possibility that they could reject cards.

While the simplest explanation for this might be fatigue—the Rorschach was administered after the WAIS—it is the examiner's impression that this accidental factor was relatively unimportant. It seems more likely that the Rorschach situation aroused anxiety in response to the danger of genuine emotional contact with each other. (They hardly seemed to listen to each other's responses on most cards.) Of the five responses they gave, four resulted from positive selection, mainly through the son's ability to accept his mother's superior responses. In this sense, the pattern does not contradict the WAIS. The actual responses tend to be rather pedestrian, with one exception (to be discussed below.) Of the five responses, none incorporate color in the determinants, while both individuals alone are quite responsive to color. Here again may be evidence of the avoidant nature of the relationship.

One of the responses in the Interaction Rorschach is so unique and possibly revealing as to deserve detailed examination.

On Card VIII, they offer: "Two bears climbing on a whale's vertebrae." This is a confabulated response. If obtained from an individual, it would possibly be considered to be pathognomonic of schizophrenia.

The individual responses to Card VIII:

Son: "This is a couple of mountain goats climbing up an extremely rough mountain."

Mother: "This looks like something out of an anatomy book. The colors are pleasant. It looks like two bears on either side here. Four legged animals. The outside looks like two animals and the center part looks like part of the spine. But a pleasant looking formation nevertheless, EVEN THOUGH IT'S A PECULIAR COMBINATION; pleasant to the eye.

Hindsight suggests that we pay close attention to this capitalized phrase in the mother's response. It seems to be just one step short of the actual contamination that emerged in Interaction Testing!

How did the two respondents arrive at the interaction response? Notes taken during their discussion (E thinks they are complete and verbatim):

Son: "Looks like two mountain goats. Or—a whale's skeleton held vertically.

Mother: It looks like bears.

Son: I guess I can see bears too.

Mother: I can see vertebrae here.

Son: It would have to be a whale's in order to hold two mountain goats.

Mother: Write vertebrae. I don't care whose vertebrae it is . . .

On the surface, this dialogue looks as though the mother, for one reason or another, yielded to her son's pathology. When we see the individual responses, however, we must wonder whether her surface acquiescence may not cover a secret victory—getting her son to express *her* pathology?

The concept of a child acting out the mother's repressed wishes is not a new one. Is this an example of it, showing the verbal process that accompanied it?

Back to our interaction analysis. We find parallels to the WAIS in that 4 of the 5 Rorschach responses occurred through selection; again suggesting minimal real contact with each other. Also, as on the WAIS, the one Emergent response is a negative one, pointing to potential destructiveness in the relationship.

In summary, the relationship between mother and son seems to be characterized by avoidance of genuine contact. It is covered by behavior in which, when conflicting judgment occurs between the two, the mother's view is generally adopted as frequently when the son's response would be superior as the other way around. Whether this reflects simple dependency or not is not determined. However, there is some reason to suspect profound unconscious collusion in which the son expresses his mother's deeper disturbance, thus helping her to avoid expressing it.

Can this be an example of a symbiotic basis for a schizophrenogenic relationship?

A Stable Homosexual Relationship

Description: A relatively stable homosexual relationship of five years duration. George, age 44, is a designer; Robert, age 41, is a writer. Both men consider their relationship to be a "good one," "better than most such relationships." George denies having any problems; Robert admits to mild periodic depressions and confusion regarding "direction in life."

An abbreviated form of the Wechsler-Bellevue I was administered, consisting of the Information, Comprehension and Similarities subtests. George and Robert took each of the tests individually and then in interaction. Their responses and scores were as follows:

INFORMATION

Item	George	Score	Robert	Score	Interaction	Score	Process
President	Eisenhower	1	Eisenhower	1	Eisenhower	1	PR
Before	Truman	1	Truman	1	Truman	1	PR
London	England	1	England	1	England	1	PR
Pints	two	1	two	1	two	1	PR
Rubber	trees	**1**	trees	**1**	trees	1	PR
Thermom.	measures temp.	1	Instrum. to meas. temp.	1	measures temp.	1	
Weeks	fifty-two	1	fifty-two	1	fifty-two	1	PR
Italy	Rome	1	Rome	1	Rome	1	PR
Wash.	Feb. 22	1	Feb. 22	1	Feb. 22	0	PR
Hght.	5'1"	0	5'4"	1	5'2"	1	NE
Plane	Wright Bros.	1	Wright	1	Wright Bros.	1	PR
Paris	2100 mi.	1	3,000 mi.	1	2500 mi.	1	PR
Brazil	S. Amer.	1	S. Amer.	1	S. Amer.	1	PR
Hamlet	Shakespeare	1	Shakespeare	1	Shakespease	0	NR
Pole	Byrd	0	Byrd	0	Byrd	0	
Vatican	Catholic Church	0	Papal State	1	Papal State	1	PS
Japan	Tokyo	1	Tokyo	1	Tokyo	1	PR
Heart	Pumps Blood	1	Pumps Blood	1	Pumps Blood	1	PR
Pop.	103 million	0	150 million	1	150 million	1	PS
H. Finn.	M. Twain	1	S. Clemens—O. Henry	0	M. Twain	1	
Egypt	Africa	1	Africa	1	Africa	1	PR
Koran	Moh. Bible	1	Scripture of Mohammedans	1	Moh. Bible	1	PR
Faust	Wagner	0	Gounod	1	Gounod	1	PS
H. Corp.	Release criminal	0	d.k.	0	Release criminal	0	NS
Ethno.	d.k.	0	d.k.	0	d.k.	0	NR
Apoc.	Doctor's oath	0	part of bible—undetermined	1	disputed part of bible	1	PS
Total: Raw Score		18		21		21	
Weighted Score		13		15		15	

COMPREHENSION

Item	George	Sc	Robert	Sc	Interaction	Sc	Process
Envelope	Mail it	2	Mail it	2	Mail it	2	PR
Theater	Look for exit	0	Tell an usher	2	Tell an usher	2	PS
Company	To stay out of trouble	1	They should not	0	To stay out of trouble	1	PS
Taxes	Support gov't.	2	Support gov't.	2	Support gov't.	2	PR
Shoes	comfort	1	durability	1	comfort durability flexibility	2	PR
Land	Real estate	0	produces	1	produces more revenue	1	PS
Forest	sun . . .	2	sun . . .	2	sun . . .	2	PR
Laws	order and protection	2	order and protection	2	order and protection	2	PR
Marriage	Legal proof	1	God knows	0	Proof	1	PS
Deaf	Learn . . . (explained)	2	Learn . . .	2	Learn	2	PR
Total: Raw Score		13		14		17	
Wtd. Score		11		12		15	

SIMILARITIES

Item	George	Sc	Robert	Sc	Interaction	Sc	Process
Orange	fruit	2	fruit	2	fruit	2	PR
Coat	clothing	2	clothing	2	clothing	2	PR
Dog	animals	2	animal	2	animals	2	PR
Wagon	vehicles	2	vehicles	2	vehicles	2	PR
Paper	dk	0	communication	2	communication	2	PS
Air	mineral?	0	elements	1	elements	1	PS
Wood	dk	0	carbohydrates	0	carbohydrates	0	NR
Eye	part of body	1	sense organs	2	sense organs	2	PS
Egg	birth	1	sperm	0	sperm	0	NS
Poem	art	2	art	2	art	2	PR
Praise	treatment	0	results (explained)	2	actions?	0	NE
Fly	both grow	1	living	2	living	2	PS
Total: Raw Score		13		19		17	
Wtd. Score		11		15		14	

SUMMATION

	Information	Comprehension	Similarities	Prorated V. I.Q.
George	13	11	11	120
Robert	15	12	15	134
Interaction	15	15	14	139

The above three protocols were presented to a clinical psychologist familiar with the technique who was told that the data had been collected from members of a homosexual pair. He was invited to speculate freely from this data about the nature of the relationship. The following is his brief report:

'This is a very bright group composed of partners who are quite unlike each other intellectually. The relationship manifests less inner disturbance than does either partner alone (less inter-test scatter, higher I.Q.). The stability of the relationship is based primarily upon positive selection: on the whole it is able to select constructively from the two diverse talents within it, frequently with more reality appropriateness than is available to either partner. There may be subtle divisiveness or dissension although this does not seem too pronounced (note the presence of several Negative Selections). In the area of abstract reasoning, however, there is some evidence that the pathology of one of the partners endangers the balance and integrity of the relationship (anxiety and conflict re: homosexuality?).

George, although obtaining a lower I.Q., is conceivably no less bright than Robert. His score suffers from his "feminine," "hysterical," imprecise approach to the test. Robert's intellect has more of a "masculine," "obsessional" quality; an approach that tends to be rewarded on such a test. The data suggest that this relationship, though not electrifyingly creative, does make fairly constructive use of its resources through selective amalgamation and division of psychic responsibility. Apparently George depends upon Robert's more precise approach in helping to shape policy for their more practical reality dealings, while Robert, who seems actively conflicted about his sexual role (note marriage item: "God knows!"), allows George to handle "public relations" for the two of them."

A Therapy Group at Two Points in Treatment

Background

An 8-member outpatient group composed of 4 men and 4 women, ranging in age from 25-40, was seen for Interaction Testing prior to the first group meeting, but after each member had been interviewed individually by the therapist. They were retested 9 months later, during which interval they had met weekly. All members are at least of average intelligence. There are no organic or psychotic members.

Tests Administered

1) *Interaction Wechsler-Bellevue* (Comprehension, Information and Similarities.

2) *Interaction Rorschach:* the Harrower Multiple Choice Test (7) was used.

Test Data

For purposes of this exposition, only the interaction product (group as a whole) will be presented.

1) *Wechsler-Bellevue*—changes in Interaction product from test to retest (9 month interval)

Information

Original testing: Raw score 21: the group failed on the last 4 items.

Retest: Raw score 23; failure on last 2 items.

Comprehension

Test: Raw score 15

Retest: Raw Score 18

Response Changes: "Shoes." Change is from 2 to 3 qualities: add 1 point

"Marriage"   Test: "Make sure qualified for marriage"
                Retest: "for records and control":
                                        add 2 points

Similarities

                    Test: Raw Score 20

                Retest: Raw Score 23

"Paper-Radio"   Test: News

                Retest: Communication.   Add 1 point

"Praise-Punishment" Test: Expression of feeling

                Retest: Discipline.   Add 2 points

Summary of Scores

	Comprehension Wtd. Score	Similarities Wtd. Score	Inf- Wtd. Score	Pro-rated Verbal I.Q.
Test	13	16	15	131
Retest	16	18	16	145

RORSCHACH

Test I	Re-Test
Card 1 A bat	An army or navy emblem
A butterfly flying	can't agree
A moth	can't agree
Card 2 *Two scottie dogs*	*Two scottie dogs*
Two bears rubbing noses	Two people playing pattycake
Bears' heads	*Bears' heads*
Card 3 *Two men pulling something apart*	*Two men pulling something apart*
Two cannibals	*Two cannibals*
Nothing at all	Two waiters bowing
Card 4 *A pair of boots*	*A pair of boots*
Charlie Chaplin's feet	*Charlie Chaplin's feet*
Big overshoes	*Big overshoes*
Card 5 *A moth*	*A moth*
A bird flying	*A bird flying*
A bat or butterfly	A fan dancer
Card 6 A totem pole	can't agree
An animal skin	can't agree
Feathers at the top	can't agree
Card 7 *Two women talking*	*Two women talking*
Indians with feathered caps	*Indians with feathered caps*
Children playing	*Children playing*
Card 8 *Two bears climbing*	*Two bears climbing*
Two animals climbing	can't agree
Two beavers walking on colored rocks	*Two beavers walking on colored rocks*
Card 9 Sea horses	can't agree
A fountain	can't agree
An explosion	can't agree
Card 10 *Spiders, caterpillars, insects*	*Spiders, caterpillars, insects*
Undersea pictures	*Undersea pictures*
Octopus and crabs	Coral and seaweed

Brief Interpretive Comments

Perhaps the most striking aspects of this data on 8 people who had never met before original testing is the consistency of test-retest responses in Interaction Testing. This finding points to probable significant reliability of group responses in this kind of testing situation. (While this is by no means a true test of reliability, it seems to be suggestive.)

Our speculations about significance of test-retest changes seem to correlate with the therapist's clinical impressions. As is typical of such groups, this therapy group was initially quite evasive and defensive, manifesting a very cautious approach to revelation of their problems. This may be reflected in the relatively non-committal, "popular" Rorschach that was elicited initially.

After 9 months, this was a group that had begun to wrestle seriously with its problems. While it had then, in a sense, become much more of a work oriented therapy group than it had been at the initial testing, it had not yet reached the level of cohesion that can be anticipated when it has begun to resolve some of its more serious problems.

The Wechsler changes seem to indicate this, in the intellectual area. The group is now more effective in using its inherent intellectual resources. (We are assuming that the change in scores is *not* due to retest effects.)

On the Rorschach, on the other hand, we see what seem to be evidences of increased internal conflict, and freedom to express it, as well as the expression of some relatively less inhibited responses. The Rorschach changes would appear to be consistent with a group which is gradually relinquishing its socially oriented "friendly" facade, in order to begin to grapple with its inner problems. This seems to be reflected in their increased ability to tolerate frustration and anxiety, and their unwillingness to comply superficially in the absence of genuine agreement.

Summary

In the foregoing we have described Interaction Testing and demonstrated its application to small groups by presenting illustrative data from our clinical work.

In summarizing we would like to stress the seemingly unique kinds of data made available through Interaction Testing.

1. Data concerning the specific interaction process in terms of health as well as pathology.
2. Data concerning the intellectual and personality characteristics of a group.
3. Data concerning the effect the group has on the intellectual and personality characteristics of the individual in it.

In addition we have described operationally three categories of interaction (i.e., emergence, selection and reinforcement) which are now amenable to quantitative and qualitative evaluation, thereby making available significantly new data for both diagnosis and research. Extensive research necessary for evaluating reliability and validity is being organized.*

While techniques for handling the data need further refinement, Interaction Testing already produces information which can be relevant and useful in the exploration of such questions as:

1. What are the dimensions by which small groups can be characterized, and which of these dimensions are most relevant to the prediction of group behavior?
2. In what ways do these dimensions vary in the life history of a group, that is, from its "birth" to its "death"?
3. Assuming that groups can be characterized as discrete and independent entities, what are the significant relationships between the characteristics of the group-as-a-group and those of its individual members with reference to such factors as personality, intelligence. productivity, creativity, etc.?

---

* Efforts to explore reliability and validity are being pursued in several areas: family diagnosis, marriage counseling, pre-adoption consultation and industrial selection and development.

4. In what ways must the assumption of individual - group psychological isomorphism be refined in order to maximize its validity?

In conclusion, Interaction Testing:

evaluates the psychological process and product of the interaction of two or more people;

evaluates the psychological characteristics of a group-as-a group;

is applicable to any small group.

Bibliography

1. Bales, R. F.: *Interaction Process Analysis.* Cambridge: Addison-Wesley, 1950.
2. Bion, W. R.: Group dynamics: a review. *International Journal of Psychoanalysis,* 33, 1952.
3. Cattell, R. B.: *The Description and Measurement of Personality.* New York: World Book, 1946.
4. Cattell, R. B.: Concepts and methods in the measurement of group syntality. *Psychological Review,* 55, 1948.
5. Davidson, H. H.: A measure of adjustment obtained from the Rorschach protocol. *Journal of Projective Techniques,* 14, 1950.
6. Gurwitch, A.: *The Sociology of Law.* New York: Philosophical Library, 1942.
7. Harrower, M. R. and Steiner, M. E.: *Large Scale Rorschach Techniques.* Springfield: Charles C Thomas, 1951.
8. Henry, W. E., and Guetzkow, H.: Group projection sketches for the study of small groups. *Journal of Social Psychology,* 33, 1951.
9. Horwitz, M. and Cartwright, D.: A projective method for the diagnosis of groups. *Human Relations,* 4, 1951.
10. Lewin, K.: *A Dynamic Theory of Personality.* New York: McGraw-Hill, 1936.
11. McDougall, W.: *The Group Mind.* New York: Putnam, 1920.
12. Sprout, H. and Sprout, M.: Environmental factors in the study of international politics. *Conflict Resolution,* 1, 1957.